BE OBE

Be Obedient

WARREN W. WIERSBE

The Bible Teacher's Teacher

An Imprint of Cook Communications Ministries
COLORADO SPRINGS, COLORADO • PARIS, ONTARIO
KINGSWAY COMMUNICATIONS, LTD., EASTBOURNE, ENGLAND

Victor® is an imprint of
Cook Communications Ministries, Colorado Springs, CO 80918
Cook Communications, Paris, Ontario
Kingsway Communications, Eastbourne, England

BE OBEDIENT
© 1991 by SP Publications, Inc.
© 2004 by Cook Communications Ministries

7 8 9 10 11   Printing/Year   08 07 06 05 04

Printed in the United States of America
Cover Photo: Digital Vision Ltd
Study Questions by Mary Tucker

Unless otherwise noted, Scripture quotations are from the *Authorized (King
James) Version.* Other quotations are from the *New American Standard Bible*
(NASB), © the Lockman Foundation 1960, 1962, 1963, 1968, 1971, 1972,
1973, 1975, 1977; the *Holy Bible, New International Version* (NIV), © 1973,
1978, 1984, International Bible Society. Used by permission of Zondervan
Bible Publishers; *The New Testament in Modern English,* Revised Edition
(PH), © J.B. Phillips, 1958, 1960, 1972, permission of Macmillan
Publishing Co. and Collins Publishers; *The New King James Version* (NKJV).
© 1979, 1980, 1982, Thomas Nelson, Inc., Publishers; *The Living Bible*
(TLB), © 1971, Tyndale House Publishers, Wheaton, IL 60189; *The New
Testament: An Expanded Translation* (WUEST) by Kenneth S. Wuest. © 1961
by the Wm. B. Eerdmans Publishing Company. Used by permission; and
the *New English Bible* (NEB), © 1961, 1970, Oxford University Press,
Cambridge University Press.

Library of Congress Cataloging-in-Publication Data

Wiersbe, Warren W.
  Be obedient / by Warren W. Wiersbe.
    p.   cm.
  ISBN 0-89693-875-1
  1. Bible. O.T. Genesis XII-XXV--Criticism, interpretation, etc.
  2. Abraham (Biblical patriarch) 3. Patriarchs (Bible)--Biography.
  4. Abraham (Biblical patriarch) I. Title.
  BS1235.2.W457 1991
  222.11092--dc20   90-29301
                                                              CIP

CONTENTS

Dedicated with affection and appreciation to

Gordon and Gail MacDonald

who walk by faith,

serve in love,

and bring hope to many who are struggling
on the path of faith.

We thank God for your friendship
and your ministry.

PREFACE

In a world filled with insecurity and uncertainty, we must learn to walk by faith, or our lives will fall apart. This applies to *all* of God's children, regardless of how old we are or how long we have walked with the Lord.

Living by faith means obeying God's Word in spite of feelings, circumstances, or consequences. It means holding on to God's truth no matter how heavy the burden or how dark the day, knowing that He is working out His perfect plan.

It means living by promises and not by explanations.

Abraham and Sarah are excellent teachers in the "School of Faith," and we are going to learn from them as we study Genesis 12–25 together. But faith is not something we study; it's something we practice. "By faith Abraham . . . *obeyed*" (Heb. 11:8; italics mine). If you want your faith to grow, be obedient!

While I was writing this book, my wife and I experienced some unexpected and painful tests of faith. As we prayed and meditated on the Word, we received the confidence and peace that God gives when you trust Him; and our own faith has been strengthened.

As you study *Be Obedient,* your faith may be tested as ours was; but don't be afraid! Remember the words of Job: "But He knows the way that I take; when He has tested me, I will come forth as gold" (Job 23:10, NIV).

Warren W. Wiersbe

ONE

A New Beginning

If the other planets are inhabited," quipped George Bernard Shaw, "then they must be using the earth for their insane asylum."

We may chuckle at that statement, but it reminds us of a sad fact: The world is in a mess, and it does not seem to be getting any better. What is wrong?

It all goes back to events recorded in the Book of Genesis. Except for the account in chapters 1 and 2, the first eleven chapters of Genesis record one failure of man after another, failures that are being repeated today. The first man and woman disobeyed God and were cast out of the Garden (chap. 3). Cain murdered his brother Abel and lied about it (chap. 4). Humanity became so corrupt that God cleansed the earth with a flood (chaps. 6–8). Noah got drunk and exposed himself to his son Ham (chap. 9). In their defiance of God, men built a city and a tower; and God had to send confusion to end the rebellion (chap. 10).

Disobedience, murder, deception, drunkenness, nudity, and rebellion sound pretty up-to-date, don't they? If you were God, what would you do with these sinners, men and women you had created in your own image?

"I'd probably destroy them!" you might reply; but that's not what God did. Instead, God called a man and his wife to leave their home and go to a new land, so that He might give humanity a new beginning. Because of God's call and their obedient faith, Abraham and Sarah* ultimately gave to the world the Jewish nation, the Bible, and the Savior. Where would we be today if Abraham and Sarah had not trusted God?

Consider the elements involved in their experience.

1. A call (Gen. 12:1a)

When God called. Salvation comes because God calls in grace and sinners respond by faith (Eph. 2:8-9; 2 Thes. 2:13-14). God called Abraham out of idolatry (Josh. 24:2), when he was in Ur of the Chaldees (Gen. 11:28, 31; 15:7; Neh. 9:7), a city devoted to Nannar, the moon-god. Abraham did not know the true God, and had done nothing to deserve knowing Him, but God graciously called him. "Ye have not chosen Me, but I have chosen you" (John 15:16).

Abraham was 75 years old when God called him, so age doesn't need to be an obstacle to faith. He trusted God for 100 years (Gen. 25:7); and from his experience, we today can learn how to walk by faith and live to please the Lord.

Abraham was married to Sarah, his half sister (20:12), and they were childless. Yet God used them to found a great nation! "I called him [Abraham] alone, and blessed him, and increased him" (Isa. 51:2). Why would God call such an unlikely couple for such an important task? Paul gives you the answer in 1 Corinthians 1:26-31.

God called Abraham after the Gentiles had failed and turned away from the true and living God. That process of devolution is described in Romans 1:18-32. Man originally

*Their original names were Abram and Sarai, but we will follow the example of Stephen in Acts 7:2 and use their new names (Gen. 17), since they are more familiar.

knew the true God, but he would not glorify Him or give thanks to Him for His gracious provision. Man substituted idols for the true and living God. Idolatry led to immorality and indecency; and before long, the Gentile world was so corrupt that God had to give it up (vv. 24, 26, 28). Then He called Abraham, the first Jew, and made a new beginning.

How God called. "The God of glory appeared unto our father, Abraham" (Acts 7:2). How God appeared to Abraham, we are not told; but it was the first of seven communications to Abraham recorded in Genesis. The revelation of God's glory would have shown Abraham the vanity and folly of the idol worship in Ur. Who wants to worship a dead idol when he has met the living God! First Thessalonians 1:9-10 and 2 Corinthians 4:6 describe this salvation experience.

But God also *spoke* to Abraham (Gen. 12:1-3), and the Word brought about the miracle of faith. "So then faith cometh by hearing, and hearing by the Word of God" (Rom. 10:17). It was a call to separate himself from the corruption around him, and Abraham obeyed by faith (Heb. 11:8). True faith is based on the Word of God and leads to obedience. God could not bless and use Abraham and Sarah unless they were in the place of His appointment (2 Cor. 6:14–7:1).

Lost sinners today are not likely to receive a special revelation of God's glory as did Abraham and Sarah. But they can see His glory in the lives of His people (Matt. 5:16) and hear His Word of faith when they *share* their witness. God spoke to Abraham directly, but today we hear the truth of salvation through the witness of His people (Acts 1:8).

Why God called. There are at least three reasons why God called Abraham and Sarah. In His love, God was concerned about their salvation; so He revealed His glory and shared His gracious promises. But even beyond their personal salvation was God's purpose in blessing the whole world. This was accomplished when God sent His Son into the world through the Jewish nation. Christ died for the sins of the world (1 John 2:2; 4:14) and wants His church to tell the good news to the whole world (Mark 16:15).

But there is a third reason: The life of Abraham is an example for all Christians who want to walk by faith. Abraham was saved by faith (Gen. 15:6; Rom. 4:1-5; Gal. 3:6-14) and lived by faith (Heb. 11:8-19), and his obedience was the evidence of his faith (James 2:14-26). Abraham obeyed when he did not know *where* (Heb. 11:8-10), *how* (vv. 11-12), *when* (vv. 13-16), or *why* (vv. 17-19); and so should we.

Abraham and Sarah were not perfect, but their walk was generally characterized by faith and faithfulness. When they sinned, they suffered for it; and the Lord was always ready to forgive when they repented. "The victorious Christian life," said George Morrison, "is a series of new beginnings." As you study the life of Abraham and Sarah, you will learn what faith is and how to walk by faith. You will discover that, when you trust the Lord, no test is impossible and no failure is permanent.

2. A covenant (Gen. 12:1-3)

Faith is not based on feeling, though the emotions are certainly involved (Heb. 11:7). True faith is based on the Word of God (Rom. 10:17). God spoke to Abraham and told him what He would do *for* him and *through* him if he would trust and obey. "Great lives are trained by great promises," wrote Joseph Parker; and this was certainly true of Abraham and Sarah. God's covenant gave them the faith and strength they needed for their lifelong pilgrim journey.

We are not saved by making promises to God; we are saved by believing God's promises to us. It was God who graciously gave His covenant to Abraham and he responded with faith and obedience (Heb. 11:8-10). How you respond to God's promises determines what God will do in your life.

A NEW BEGINNING

The Bible records God's many covenants, beginning with the promise of the Redeemer in Genesis 3:15 and climaxing with the New Covenant through the blood of Jesus Christ (Luke 22:20; Heb. 8). The Hebrew word translated "covenant" has several meanings: (1) *to eat with,* which suggests fellowship and agreement; (2) *to bind or fetter,* which means commitment; and (3) *to allot,* which suggests sharing. When God makes a covenant, He enters into an agreement to commit Himself to give what He promises. It is purely an act of grace.

God did not give Abraham reasons or explanations; He simply gave him promises: "I will show thee ... I will make of thee ... I will bless thee ... I will bless them that bless thee" (Gen. 12:1-2). God promised to show him a land, make him into a great nation, and use that nation to bless the whole world. God *blesses* us that we might be a *blessing* to others, and His great concern is that the whole world might be blessed. *The missionary mandate of the church does not begin with John 3:16 or Matthew 28:18-20. It begins with God's covenant with Abraham.* We are *blessed* that we might be a *blessing.*

Notice the contrast between Genesis 11:1-9 and 12:1-3. At Babel, men said, "Let us!" but to Abraham, God said, "I will." At Babel, men wanted to make a name for themselves; but it was God who made Abraham's name great. At Babel, the workers tried to unite men, only to divide them; but through Abraham, a whole world has been blessed, and all believers are united in Jesus Christ. Of course, Pentecost (Acts 2) is the "reversal" of Babel; but Pentecost could not have occurred apart from God's covenant with Abraham (Gal. 3:14).

It must have seemed incredible to Abraham and Sarah that God would bless the whole world through an elderly childless couple, but that is just what He did. From them came the nation of Israel, and from Israel came the Bible and the Savior. God reaffirmed this covenant with Isaac (Gen. 26:4) and Jacob (28:14) and fulfilled it in Christ (Acts 3:25-26). In later years, God amplified the various elements of this covenant; but He gave Abraham and Sarah sufficient truth for them to believe Him and set out by faith.

3. A compromise (Gen. 11:27-32; 12:4)

First steps of faith are not always giant steps, which explains why Abraham did not fully obey God. Instead of leaving his family, as he was commanded, Abraham took his father and his nephew Lot with him when he left Ur; and then he stayed at Haran until his father died.

Whatever you bring with you from the old life into the new is likely to create problems. Terah, Abraham's father, kept Abraham from fully obeying the Lord; and Lot created serious problems for Abraham until they finally had to agree to part. Abraham and Sarah brought a sinful agreement with them from Ur (20:13), and it got them into trouble twice (12:10-20; 20:1-18).

The life of faith demands total separation *from* what is evil and total devotion *to* what is holy (2 Cor. 6:14–7:1). As you study the life of Abraham, you will discover that he was often tempted to compromise; and occasionally he yielded. God tests us in order to build our faith and bring out the best in us, but the devil tempts us in order to destroy our faith and bring out the worst in us.

When you walk by faith, you lean on God alone: His Word, His character, His will, and His power. You don't isolate yourself from your family and friends, but you no longer consider them your first love or your first obligation (Luke 14:25-27). Your love for God is so strong that it makes family love look like hatred in comparison! God calls us "alone" (Isa. 51:1-2), and we must not compromise.

4. A commitment (Gen. 12:4-9)

The seventeenth-century Puritan preacher, Thomas Fuller, said that all mankind was divided into three classes: the intenders, the endeavorers, and the performers. Terah may have been an intender, but he never made it into the land of promise. Lot was an endeavorer up to a point, but he failed miserably because he could not walk by faith. Abraham and Sarah were the performers because they trusted God to perform what He promised (Rom. 4:18-21). They committed their lives and futures to God, obeyed what He commanded, and received all that God planned for them.

Faith brings us out (Gen. 12:4-5). It may have been a son's love for his aged father that made Abraham delay (Luke 9:59-62), but the day finally came when he and Sarah had to leave Haran and go to the land God chose for them. Faith and a double mind never go together (James 1:6-8), and you cannot serve two masters (Matt. 6:24). Faith demands commitment.

I sometimes get the impression that *commitment* is a vanishing commodity in today's world. Many people don't want to be committed to their jobs, their marriage vows, or to one another. "I'm going to do *my* thing *my* way!" is the essence of today's philosophy, and this attitude has invaded the church. Many believers will not commit themselves to ministering in one church but move from church to church when pastors and music programs change. "Temporary" is a key word today: temporary Sunday School teachers and youth sponsors, temporary choir members, temporary church members, and even temporary pastors.

"It is a day of fading declarations," said Vance Havner. "Church covenants are found in the backs of hymn books, but they have faded in the lives of most of our members—if they ever meant anything. Declarations of personal dedication grow dim, and need to be renewed. It is a day of faded declarations!"

Where would we be today if Abraham and Sarah had not committed themselves to obey the Lord by faith? Where would we be if previous generations of Christians had not given themselves fully to the Lord? We who come along later must not take for granted the things that previous generations paid a great price to attain. May the next generation look back at us and say, "They were faithful!"

Faith brings us in (Gen. 12:6-8). God brings us out that He might bring us in (Deut. 6:23). We know nothing about their long journey from Haran to Canaan, because it was the destination that was important. Centuries later, God would give that land to Abraham's descendants; but when Abraham and Sarah arrived, they were "strangers and pilgrims" in the midst of a pagan society (Heb. 11:13).

In spite of what the folk songs say, entering Canaan is not a picture of dying and going to heaven. It is a picture of the believer claiming his or her inheritance by faith. God has appointed a "Canaan" for each of His children (Eph. 2:10), and it is obtained only by faith. Claiming your inheritance involves tests and temptations, challenges and battles, but God is able to see you through (Phil. 1:6).

Obedience leads to new assurance and new promises from God (Gen. 12:7; John 7:17). What comfort it must have brought when Abraham and Sarah had this fresh revelation of God as they arrived in a strange and dangerous land. When you walk by faith, you know that God is with you and you don't need to be afraid (Heb. 13:5-6; Acts 18:9-10; 2 Tim. 4:17). God will work out His purposes and accomplish in and through you all that is in His heart.

Most of us are not commanded to pull up stakes and go to a strange country, but the challenges to our faith are just as real. Sometimes there are serious problems in the home, on the job, or in the church; and we wonder why God has permitted these things to happen. If you are to claim your spiritual inheritance in Christ, you must display faith in God's Word and obedience to God's will.

Wherever Abraham went in the land of Canaan, he was marked by his *tent* and his *altar* (Gen. 12:7-8; 13:3-4, 18). The tent marked him as a "stranger and pilgrim" who did not belong to this world (Heb. 11:9-16; 1 Peter 2:11), and the altar marked him as a citizen of heaven who worshiped the true and living God. He gave witness to all that he was separated from this world (the tent) and devoted to the Lord (the altar). Whenever Abraham abandoned his tent and his altar, he got into trouble.

Abraham pitched his tent with Bethel on the west and Ai on the east (Gen. 12:8). Bible names sometimes have significant meanings, though we must not press them too far. Bethel means "the house of God" (28:19), and Ai means "ruin." Figuratively speaking, Abraham and Sarah were walking in the light, from east to west, from the city of ruin to the house of God! This world system is in ruins, but true believers have turned their backs on this world and have set their faces toward God's heavenly home. "The path of the righteous is like the first gleam of dawn, shining ever brighter till the full light of day" (Prov. 4:18, NIV).

Faith brings us on (Gen. 12:9). The life of faith must never stand still; for if your feet are going, your faith is growing. Note the verbs used to describe Abraham's life: he departed (12:4), went forth (12:5), passed through (12:6), removed (12:8) and journeyed (12:9). God kept Abraham moving so that he would meet new challenges and be forced to trust God for new "grace to help in time of need" (Heb. 4:16). Comfortable Christianity is opposite the life of faith, for "pilgrims and strangers" must face new circumstances if they are to gain new insights about themselves and their Lord. "Let us press on to maturity" is the challenge (6:1, NASB).

How did Abraham know where to go and what to do? He

"called upon the name of the Lord" (Gen. 12:8). He prayed to the Lord, and the Lord helped him. Abraham's pagan neighbors saw that he had an altar but no idols. He had no "sacred places" but built his altar to God wherever he pitched his tent. You could trace Abraham's steps by the altars he left behind. He was not ashamed to worship God openly while his heathen neighbors watched him.

In the pilgrim life, you must go "from faith to faith" (Rom. 1:17) if you would go "from strength to strength" (Ps. 84:7). G.A. Studdert Kennedy said, "Faith is not believing in spite of evidence; it is obeying in spite of consequence." "By faith Abraham . . . obeyed" (Heb. 11:8). Faith without obedience is dead (James 2:14-26), and action without faith is sin (Rom. 14:23). God has wedded faith and obedience like the two sides of a coin; they go together.

This does not mean that sinners are saved by faith *plus* works, because Scripture declares that sinners are saved by faith alone (John 3:16-18; Eph. 2:8-9). Dr. H.A. Ironside, long-time pastor of Chicago's Moody Church, was told by a lady that she expected to get to heaven by faith plus her good works. "It's like rowing a boat," she explained. "It takes two oars to row a boat; otherwise you go around in a circle." Dr. Ironside replied, "That's a good illustration except for one thing: *I'm not going to heaven in a rowboat!*"

The faith that saves is the faith that proves itself in good works (Eph. 2:8-10; Titus 2:14; 3:8, 14). Abraham was saved by faith (Heb. 11:8; Gen. 15:6; Rom. 4:1-5), but his faith was made evident by his obedience (James 2:21-24).

Abraham is now in the place of God's appointment, doing what God told him to do. But this is not the end—it is the beginning! Even in the place of obedience you will face tests and trials, for that is how faith grows. But the same Lord who brought you *out*, brought you *in*, and brought you *on* in your pilgrim journey will also bring you *through* if you follow Him by faith.

T W O

Famines, Flocks, and Fights

L ife can be difficult," wrote Amy Carmichael, missionary to India. "Sometimes the enemy comes in like a flood. But then is the time to prove our faith and live our songs" (*Candles in the Dark,* p. 51).

A faith that can't be tested can't be trusted. Peter compared the Christian's trials to the testing of gold in the furnace (1 Peter 1:7), and the patriarch Job used the same image: "But He knows the way that I take; when He has tested me, I shall come forth as gold" (Job 23:10, NKJV). God's purpose in allowing trials is not only to verify our faith but also to purify it and remove the dross. God knows what kind of faith we have, but *we* don't know; and the only way to advance in the "school of faith" is to take examinations.

Like Abraham, as you progress in the "school of faith," you will face three special tests: *circumstances* (Gen. 12:10), *people* (12:11–13:4), and *things* (13:5-18).

1. Circumstances (Gen. 12:10)
In leaving his family and traveling to an unknown land, Abraham took a great step of faith. After he arrived, he saw God a second time and heard His word of promise. Abraham and

21

Sarah probably expected to settle down and enjoy their new home, but God would not let them. Instead, God permitted a famine to come to the land. There is no record that Abraham ever faced a famine in Ur or Haran; but now that he was in God's land, he had to find food for a large company of people, plus flocks and herds (see 14:14).

Why did God allow the famine? To teach Abraham and Sarah a basic lesson in the "school of faith," a lesson you must also learn: *Tests often follow triumphs*. This principle is illustrated in the history of Israel. No sooner had the nation been delivered from Egypt than the Egyptian army chased them and cornered them at the Red Sea (Ex. 12–15). Triumph was followed by testing. God brought them through, but then they faced another test: no water (15:22-27). After that came hunger (Ex. 16) and an attack from the Amalekites (Ex. 17). Tests follow triumphs.

"I thought that getting saved was the end of all my troubles," a young believer said to me. "But now I know that faith in Christ has given me a whole new set of problems! But now there are two differences," he added with a smile. "I don't face them alone, because the Lord is with me; and I know He allows them for my good and His glory."

One of the enemies of the life of faith is pride. When you win a victory, you may feel overconfident and start telling yourself that you can defeat *any* enemy at *any* time. You start depending on your past experience and your growing knowledge of the Word, instead of depending wholly on the Lord. This explains why the promise of 1 Corinthians 10:13 is preceded by the warning of verse 12: "Therefore let him who thinks he stands take heed lest he fall" (NKJV). God did not want Abraham to become proud and self-confident, so He put him and his faith into the furnace of testing.

After you have won a great victory of faith, expect the enemy to attack you or the Lord to test you, or both. *This is the only way you can grow in your faith.* God uses the tough circumstances of life to build the muscles of your faith and keep you from trusting something other than His Word. *Don't try to run away from the problem.* It won't work.

Instead of remaining in the land and trusting the Lord to help him, Abraham went "down into Egypt" (Gen. 12:10). In the Bible, Egypt is a symbol of the world system and its bondage, while the land of Israel is a picture of the inheritance of blessing God has for you (Deut. 11:10-12). When people went to Jerusalem, they went *up;* but when they went to Egypt, they went *down.* Spiritually speaking, "going down to Egypt" means doubting God's promises and running to the world for help. (See Num. 11; 14; Isa. 30:1-2; 31:1; and Jer. 42:13ff.)

When circumstances become difficult and you are in the furnace of testing, *remain where God has put you until He tells you to move.* Faith moves in the direction of peace and hope, but unbelief moves in the direction of restlessness and fear. "He that believeth shall not make haste" (Isa. 28:16). In times of testing, the important question is not, *"How* can I get out of this?" but, *"What* can I get out of this?" (See James 1:1-12.) God is at work to build your faith.

God alone is in control of circumstances. You are safer in a famine *in His will* than in a palace *out of His will.* It has well been said, "The will of God will never lead you where the grace of God cannot keep you." Abraham failed the test of circumstances and turned from the will of God.

2. People (Gen. 12:11–13:4)
Once in Egypt, Abraham faced a new set of problems; for if you run away from one test, you will soon face another. Once you enroll in "the school of faith," you are not allowed to "drop out" just because of one failure. God has purposes to fulfill in you and through you, and He will do all that is

necessary to make you succeed (Ps. 138:8; Phil. 1:6).

In Canaan, all Abraham had to deal with was a famine; but in Egypt, he had to get along with a proud ruler and his officers. Pharaoh was looked on as a god, but he was not a god like Abraham's God, loving and generous and faithful. Abraham soon discovered that he had been better off dealing with the circumstances in Canaan than with the people in Egypt. Notice the changes that took place in Abraham's life because he went down to Egypt.

To begin with, *Abraham moved from trusting to scheming.* Abraham had no altar in Egypt, and you don't find him calling on the Lord for guidance and help. When I was ministering in Youth for Christ International, my friend and fellow worker Pete Quist often reminded us, "Faith is living without scheming." When you stop trusting God's Word, you start leaning on man's wisdom; and this leads to trouble (Prov. 3:5-6; 1 Cor. 3:18-20). Abraham and Sarah brought this "half-truth" with them from Ur (Gen. 20:13), used it in Egypt and Gerar (Gen. 20), and then their son Isaac adopted it (Gen. 26). When you find yourself scheming in order to escape problems with people, beware; worse trouble is coming!

He also moved *from confidence to fear.* When you are in the place of God's choosing, you don't ever need to be afraid; for faith and fear cannot dwell in the same heart (Isa. 12:2; Mark 4:40). The fear of God is the fear that conquers every fear (Ps. 112; Isa. 8:13); but "the fear of man brings a snare" (Prov. 29:25, NKJV). God had repeatedly said "I will" to Abraham, but now Abraham was saying *"They* will" (Gen. 12:12, italics added). He took his eyes off the Lord and started looking at people.

A third change took place: *He moved from "others" to self.* He lied so that it might "be well with me for thy [Sarah's] sake" (12:13). As the husband, Abraham should have thought first of his wife and not of himself (1 Peter 3:7; Eph. 5:25, 28-

29). In fact, he should never have taken his wife there in the first place! A husband out of the will of God can bring untold trouble to his wife and family.

This leads to a fourth change: *He moved from bringing blessing to bringing judgment.* God called Abraham to be a blessing to the nations (Gen. 12:1-3); but because of Abraham's disobedience, judgment fell on Pharaoh and his household (12:17). This also happened years later in Gerar (Gen. 20). If you want to be a blessing to others, then stay in the will of God. Jonah ran from God's will and caused a storm that almost sank the ship. Like Jonah, Abraham lost his testimony before unbelievers and had to face embarrassment and rebuke.

God graciously watched over His servant and brought him out of a difficult situation. If Sarah had become one of Pharaoh's wives, what would have happened to the promise of the Redeemer? When we don't let God rule, He overrules and accomplishes His purposes; but we pay dearly for our disobedience.

Abraham learned his lesson, repented, and "went up" out of Egypt (13:1). When you disobey the will of God, the only right thing to do is to go back to the place where you left Him and make a new beginning (1 John 1:9). *No failure is permanent in "the school of faith."* Abraham went back to his tent and altar and the life of a "pilgrim and stranger."

A casual observer of this episode might conclude, "What happened to Abraham wasn't all bad. Pharaoh gave Abraham a lot of wealth (Gen. 12:16; 13:2), and Sarah was given her own maid, Hagar (16:1). God forgave Abraham's sin, and he started over again. So, what's the big problem?"

The "big problem" is that *everything Abraham received in Egypt later caused trouble.* Because of their great wealth, Abraham and Lot could not live together and had to separate (13:5-6). Hagar, the Egyptian maidservant, brought division and sorrow into the home (Gen. 16). Having had a taste of Egypt (the world), Lot started measuring everything by what he saw there (13:10-11); and this led to his downfall and the ruin of his family. There are no benefits from disobedience.

The practical lesson from all of this is simply *never abandon your altar.* Stay in fellowship with the Lord no matter what the circumstances may be. If you have disobeyed and God is disciplining you, *go back to the place where you left Him and make things right.* Remember: "The victorious Christian life is a series of new beginnings." That is not an excuse for sin, but it is an encouragement for repentance.

3. Things (Gen. 13:5-18)

I wonder how many family fights have been caused by the love of money. The newspapers often publish reports about families battling in court because of an inheritance or a lottery winning. People who used to love each other and enjoy each other start attacking each other just to get money, *but money cannot buy the blessings that families freely give.*

Abraham may have failed the first two tests, but he passed this third test with great success. The test was not an easy one, for it involved land and wealth; but Abraham is the example of what every believer should do when there are disputes about material things.

Abraham determined to be a peacemaker and not a trouble-maker. The problem between Abraham and Lot was not caused by the land, the famine, their wealth (both of them were rich), or even their herdsmen (13:7). *The heart of every problem is the problem in the heart.* Lot's heart was centered on wealth and worldly achievement, while Abraham wanted only to please the Lord. "Can two walk together, except they be agreed?" (Amos 3:3)

It was bad enough that this dispute was between brethren (Gen. 13:8); but even worse, the heathen people of the land

26

were watching and listening (13:7). *When Christians have disputes, it hurts the testimony of the Lord.* In my pastoral ministry, I frequently visited the unsaved relatives and friends of church members, seeking to interest them in spiritual things, only to discover that they knew about every "church fight" in town. No wonder our Lord prayed that His people might be one, that the world might believe (John 17:20-23). Christian unity is fragrant and fruitful (Ps. 133), but disunity turns that fragrance into a stench and the garden into a desert.

James 3:13–4:10 explains why Lot was a troublemaker instead of a peacemaker: He had "heart trouble." He followed the wisdom of this world (as Uncle Abraham had done in Egypt) and not God's wisdom. He was at war with Abraham because he was at war with himself, and he was at war with himself because he was at war with God. The world's wisdom and the world's wealth seem so satisfying, but they ultimately bring disappointment.

Covetousness—an insatiable appetite for more things—leads to all kinds of evil (1 Tim. 6:10). In order to get more money, people will lie (Prov. 21:6), mistreat people (22:16), cheat (28:8), and even trouble their own families (15:27). "Covetousness is both the beginning and the end of the devil's alphabet," wrote Robert South, "the first vice in corrupt nature that moves, and the last which dies."

Abraham had caused trouble in Egypt because he was out of place, and Lot caused trouble in Canaan because he was out of place: *His heart was really in Egypt* (13:10). According to 1 Corinthians 2:14–3:3, there are only three kinds of people in the world: the natural (unsaved), the carnal (saved but living for the world and the flesh), and the spiritual (devoted to God). You find all three in Genesis 13: the natural (13:13), the carnal (Lot), and the spiritual (Abraham). Lot was a righteous man (2 Peter 2:7-8) but not devoted to the Lord. He could not walk with Abraham because Abraham was the friend of God (2 Chron. 20:7; Isa. 41:8) and Lot was a friend of the world (James 4:4). Many church splits and family fights are caused by carnal Christians who are not walking with the Lord or with other believers.

Abraham lived for others, not for self. While in Egypt, Abraham thought first about himself (Gen. 12:12-13); but when he returned to his altar in Canaan, he put God first and others next. As the "elder statesman" of the camp, Abraham had every right to decide the issue and tell Lot what to do; but he gave Lot first choice. "Be kindly affectioned one to another with brotherly love, in honor preferring one another" (Rom. 12:10). The spiritual Christian does not insist on his or her own rights but gladly yields to others.

In his latter years, General William Booth, founder of the Salvation Army, was too infirm to attend the Army's world conference; but he would send the delegates a message. One year he cabled them only one word: OTHERS. I have been privileged to minister with the Salvation Army in different parts of the world, and I can testify that they take that word OTHERS very seriously. "Each of you should look not only to your own interests, but also to the interests of others" (Phil. 2:4, NIV).

Abraham lived by faith, not by sight. No matter what Lot did, Abraham was not worried about his future; for he knew that everything was in the hands of the Lord. Abraham had never read Psalm 47:4 or Matthew 6:33, but he was putting both into practice by faith. He had met God at the altar and he knew that everything was under control. *When God is first in your life, it makes no difference who is second or last.*

Lot had a tent but no altar (Gen. 13:5), which meant he did not call on the Lord for wisdom in making decisions (James 1:5). Instead of lifting up his eyes to heaven, Lot lifted up his eyes to the plain of Jordan (Gen. 13:10) and stopped there. *The eyes see what the heart loves.* Abraham had taken Lot out of Egypt, but he could not take Egypt out of Lot. Outlook helps to determine outcome. Abraham's eyes were on the holy city of God (Heb. 11:13-16), and he went on to walk with the Lord and inherit blessing. Lot's eyes were on the sinful cities of men, and he went on to worldly success, spiritual failure, and a shameful end.

Lot had a great opportunity to become a man of God as he walked with Abraham, but we don't read of Lot's building an altar or calling on the Lord. First, Lot looked toward Sodom (Gen. 13:10); then he moved toward Sodom (13:11-12); and finally, he moved into Sodom (14:12). Instead of being a pilgrim who made progress, Lot regressed into the world and away from God's blessing (Ps. 1:1). He "journeyed east" (Gen. 13:11) and turned his back on Bethel ("house of God") and toward Ai ("ruins"; see 12:8). The people in Sodom may not have appeared wicked to Lot, but they were wicked as far as God was concerned; and His evaluation is all that matters.

Abraham let God choose for him. After Lot had gone away, Abraham had another meeting with the Lord (13:14-18). Lot had lifted up his eyes and seen what the world had to offer; now God invited Abraham to lift up his eyes and see what heaven had to offer. Lot chose a piece of land which he finally lost, but God gave Abraham *the whole land which still belongs to him and his descendants.* Lot had said, "I will take." God said to Abraham, "I will give." What a contrast!

Lot lost his family, but Abraham was promised a family so large it could not be counted. (Remember, Abraham and Sarah were old and had no children.) Lot was living for the possible, but Abraham was trusting God for the impossible.

"Lift up your eyes and look" was followed by "Lift up your feet and walk" (see 13:17). Claim your inheritance by faith! (Josh. 1:1-3; Deut. 11:24) The discipline he experienced in going down to Egypt had taught Abraham to respect boundaries, so now God could trust him with horizons. *It is your faith in God that determines how much of His blessing you will enjoy.*

When you trusted Jesus Christ as your Savior, God gave you "all spiritual blessings in heavenly places in Christ" (Eph. 1:3). You now have your inheritance! All you need do is appropriate that inheritance by faith and draw on "His riches in glory" (Phil. 4:19). The Word of God is the "will" that tells you how rich you are, and faith is the key that opens the vault so you can claim your inheritance.

Abraham gave thanks to God. Not only did Abraham lift up his eyes and look (Gen. 13:14) and lift up his feet and walk (13:17), but he also lifted up his heart and worshiped God and thanked Him for His gracious blessing. He pitched his tent from place to place as God led him, and he built his altar of witness and worship. The people in Sodom were proud of their affluence (Ezek. 16:49), but Abraham had spiritual wealth that they knew nothing about (John 4:31-34). He was walking in fellowship with God, and his heart was satisfied.

Satan wants to use circumstances, people, and things to tempt you and bring out the worst in you; but God also wants to use them to test you and bring out the best in you. Abraham failed the first two tests because he resorted to faith in man's wisdom instead of faith in God's Word. But he passed the third test with great distinction because he let God take control. "And this is the victory that has overcome the world—our faith" (1 John 5:4, NKJV).

THREE

Faith Is the Victory

When you enroll in the "school of faith," you never know what may happen next. Visit Abraham one day and you find him settling a boundary dispute. Visit him another day and you see him gearing up for a battle. Why is this so?

For one thing, God wants us to mature in every area of life, but maturity doesn't come easily. There can be no growth without challenge, and there can be no challenge without change. If circumstances never changed, everything would be predictable; and the more predictable life becomes, the less challenge it presents. William Cullen Bryant wrote:

Weep not that the world changes—did it keep
A stable changeless state, 'twere cause indeed to weep.

When you walk in the light (1 John 1:5-10), you can see what is going on, and you experience variety in your life. But in the darkness, everything looks alike. No wonder unsaved people (and backslidden believers) are so bored and must constantly seek escape! The life of faith presents challenges that keep you going—and keep you growing!

In this chapter, Abraham, the man of faith, fulfills three

31

special roles: the watcher (Gen. 14:1-12), the warrior (vv. 13-16), and the worshiper (vv. 17-24). In all three roles, Abraham exercised faith in God and made the right decisions.

1. Abraham the watcher (Gen. 14:1-12)

This section records the first war mentioned in the Bible, and it would not be included here had it not involved Abraham. The Bible records a great deal of history; but, as Dr. A.T. Pierson said, "History is His story." What is written helps us better understand how God worked out His great plan of salvation in this world. In the Bible, historical facts are often windows for spiritual truth.

The five city-states in the plain of Jordan (14:2; see 13:10) had been subject for twelve years to the kings of four eastern city-states (14:1) and finally revolted against them. This, of course, was a declaration of war; so the four kings invaded the plain of Jordan to bring the five kings into subjection. From our modern viewpoint, the invasion was a minor skirmish; but in that day, it was considered a major international conflict.

Certainly five kings ought to be able to defeat four kings, especially when they are fighting "on their own turf." But the army of the cities of the plain was soundly defeated by the invading kings! Apparently the five kings did not even know their own land because they were trapped in the slime pits (14:10). All their army could do was flee for the hills.

While reviewing his troops, the Duke of Wellington is supposed to have said, "I don't know what effect these men will have on the enemy, but they frighten *me!*" Ezekiel 16:49-50 suggests that the lifestyle of the people of Sodom and Gomorrah did not prepare them for conflict. (Cf. Ezek. 16:49-50 with 1 John 2:15-17.)

Whatever purposes the kings may have had in this war, God had something special in mind for Lot: he became a prisoner of war. Lot had *looked at* Sodom and *moved toward* Sodom (Gen. 13:10-13), and now he was *living in* Sodom (14:12; see Ps. 1:1). You might not guess it from his conduct, but Lot was a righteous man (2 Peter 2:6-8). Where did he fail?

While in Egypt with Abraham, Lot had gotten a taste of the world and enjoyed it. Scripture doesn't record that Lot ever built an altar and sought the Lord, as did his uncle Abraham. Abraham was the friend of God (James 2:23), but Lot was the friend of the world (4:4). In time, Lot conformed to the world (Rom. 12:2); and when Sodom lost the war, Lot was condemned with the world (1 Cor. 11:32). If you identify with the world, then expect to suffer what the world suffers.

Lot's capture was God's way of disciplining him and reminding him that he had no business living in Sodom. No doubt Abraham was praying faithfully for his nephew that he might separate himself from the world and start living like a true "stranger and pilgrim." God disciplines His children because He loves them and wants the best for them (Prov. 3:11-12; Heb. 12:1-11). If we don't listen to His rebukes, then He has to get our attention some other way; and that way is usually very painful.

2. Abraham the warrior (Gen. 14:13-16)

His attitude. Abraham did not get involved in the war until he heard that Lot had been captured, and then he began to act. *Abraham was separated, but not isolated; he was independent, but not indifferent.* In fact, he and some of the local sheiks had formed an alliance for just such emergencies (14:13). He was "Abram, the Hebrew" (14:13), which means "the outsider, the person with no secure place in society." He was not "Abraham the hardhearted." He was a "pilgrim and stranger" in the land, but that was no excuse for inaction.

While believers must not compromise with the unsaved in

matters of spiritual walk and ministry (2 Cor. 6:14–7:1), they may cooperate when it comes to caring for humanity and "promoting the general welfare." When you see that people are in trouble, you don't ask them for a testimony before helping them (Luke 10:25-37; Gal. 6:10). Sacrificial service is one way of showing the love of Christ to others (Matt. 5:16). If Christians don't carry their share of the common burdens of life, how can they be the salt of the earth and the light of the world?

For example, Joseph served in Egypt, and God used him to preserve his family and the Jewish nation. Nehemiah served a heathen king, yet God used the authority and resources of that king to enable Nehemiah to rebuild Jerusalem. Esther was a Jewess married to a Gentile ruler, and God used her to protect the Jewish people from almost certain annihilation. Daniel in Babylon never compromised his convictions, but he did assist several rulers and was greatly used by God. We may cooperate with different people at different times to achieve different purposes, but we should always be conscious of our obligation to glorify God.

Abraham treated his nephew with love, both when he gave Lot first choice of the land (Gen. 13:9) and when he risked his own life to rescue him. Lot had not been kind to Abraham, and Abraham had every excuse to let his nephew suffer the painful consequences of his own stupid decisions. But Lot was his "brother" (14:16), so Abraham practiced brotherly love and overcame evil with good (Rom. 12:17-21; Gal. 6:1-2).

His army. Though a man of peace, Abraham was prepared for war. He didn't fight from selfish motives to get personal gain; he fought because he loved Lot and wanted to help him. When you consider the characteristics of Abraham's army, you see what it takes in the spiritual realm to have victory over the world.

(1) They were born in his house (v. 14). Spiritually speaking,

this reminds us that "whatever is born of God overcomes the world" (1 John 5:4, NKJV). Our first birth made us children of Adam, and he was a loser; but our second birth makes us children of God, and Jesus Christ is the Victor. He has overcome every enemy (Eph. 1:19-23), and He shares His victory with all who will trust Him. "And this is the victory that has overcome the world—our faith" (1 John 5:4, NKJV).

(2) They were armed (v. 14). It takes more than zeal and courage to win a war: You must also have effective equipment. The Christian soldier must wear the whole armor of God and use the spiritual weapons God has provided (Eph. 6:10-18). Our weapons are spiritual, not fleshly (2 Cor. 10:3-5); and we use them in the power of the Holy Spirit. The Word of God and prayer are our two most effective weapons (Acts 6:4), and we must use them by faith. As the well-known song expresses it: "Put on the Gospel armor/Each piece put on with prayer."

(3) They were trained (v. 14). No matter how good their equipment is, if the soldiers are not trained, they will be easily defeated. One of the purposes of the local church is to train God's people how to use the Bible effectively, how to pray, how to recognize the enemy, and how to follow orders as soldiers in the army of Christ. *The better you know your Bible, the better you are equipped to fight the battle* (2 Tim. 3:16-17). The Captain of your salvation wants to train you and "make you perfect [complete]" (Heb. 13:20-21), and the Greek word means "to equip an army." If we fail in the battle, it is not the fault of the equipment or the strategy of our Captain. Something is wrong with the soldiers.

(4) They believed in their leader. Abraham and his allies rode 120 miles to make a surprise attack on the four kings, and they won a complete victory. Apparently Abraham got his directions from the Lord, so the whole enterprise was a victory of faith. The spiritual application is clear: If God's people

expect to defeat their enemies, they must trust the Lord and obey His orders. This is how Joshua conquered the Promised Land and David defeated the enemies of Israel, and this is the way the church must fight today.

(5) They were united. There were not three armies with three leaders; there was one army, and Abraham was in charge. If God's people today were united in love, what victories we would win! We sing, "Like a mighty army/Moves the church of God"; but the church is very unlike an army, especially when it comes to the discipline of marching together. "The trouble with the church," said a pastor friend, "is that there are too many generals and not enough privates!"

(6) They were single-minded. Their goal was not personal revenge or private gain (Gen. 14:22-23), but victory over the enemy so that the captives might be freed. A double-minded soldier is destined for defeat. "No one engaged in warfare entangles himself with the affairs of this life, that he may please him who enlisted him as a soldier" (2 Tim. 2:4, NKJV). When you remember Achan (Josh. 7), Samson (Jud. 13–16), and Saul (1 Sam. 15), you see how true that statement is.

His achievement. Abraham and his allies were so strong that they chased the enemy for 100 miles, freed all the captives, and recovered all the spoils. Did Abraham and his worldly nephew have a long talk as they rode back? Did Lot keep the promises he made while he was in danger? Did he make any promises to Abraham?

We cannot answer those questions, but we do know this: Neither the Lord's chastening nor the Lord's goodness in rescuing Lot did him any good. The goodness of God should have led him to repentance (Luke 15:14-19; Rom. 2:4); but instead of repenting, Lot returned to Sodom. He could have been reunited with Abraham, but he chose to go back to sin.

"Abraham was the father of the faithful," wrote Alexander

Whyte in his classic *Bible Characters*. "And Lot, his nephew, was the father of all such as are scarcely saved." Some will be saved "so as by fire" (1 Cor. 3:15), but it is far better to have "an abundant entrance" into the Lord's everlasting kingdom (2 Peter 1:11).

3. Abraham the worshiper (Gen. 14:17-24)

A new battle. Sometimes you face your greatest dangers after you have won a battle. It was after the capture of Jericho that Israel's self-confidence led it into defeat at Ai (Josh. 7); and after his success on Mount Carmel, Elijah panicked and ran away in fear (1 Kings 19). No wonder the saintly Scottish pastor Andrew Bonar (1810–1892) said, "Let us be as watchful after the victory as before the battle."

When Abraham returned from battle, he was met by two kings: Bera, King of Sodom ("burning"), and Melchizedek, King of Salem ("peace"). Bera offered Abraham all the spoils in return for the people, while Melchizedek gave Abraham bread and wine. Abraham rejected Bera's offer but accepted the bread and wine from Melchizedek and gave him tithes of the spoils. All of this is symbolic and presents some important spiritual truths that you should understand and apply today.

Abraham had to choose between two kings who represented two opposite ways of life. Sodom was a wicked city (Gen. 13:13; Ezek. 16:49-50), and Bera represented the dominion of this world system with its appeal to the flesh (Eph. 2:1-3). Bera means "gift," suggesting that the world bargains for your allegiance. But Sodom means "burning," so be careful how you choose! If you bow down to Bera, everything you live for will burn up one day. That's what happened to Lot!

Melchizedek means "king of righteousness," and Salem means "peace." Hebrews 7 and Psalm 110 both connect Melchizedek with Jesus Christ, the "King of peace" and the

"King of righteousness" (85:10). Like Melchizedek in Abraham's day, Jesus Christ is our King-Priest in heaven, enabling us to enjoy righteousness and peace as we serve Him (Isa. 32:17; Heb. 12:11). Certainly we can see in the bread and wine a reminder of our Lord's death for us on the cross.

So, when Abraham rejected Bera and accepted Melchizedek, he was making a statement of faith, saying, "Take the world, but give me Jesus." Lot should have made the same decision, but he chose to return to his life of compromise.

Why would it have been wrong for Abraham to take the spoils? After all, didn't he risk his life and the lives of his retainers to defeat the invading kings and rescue the prisoners? Legally, Abraham had every claim to the spoils; but morally, they were out of bounds. *Many things in this world are legal as far as courts are concerned but morally wrong as far as God's people are concerned.*

Furthermore, before Abraham could take the spoils, he had to agree to restore the people of Sodom to their king who said, "Give me the persons" (Gen. 14:21). Just as God wants to use human bodies for His glory (Rom. 12:1-2; 1 Cor. 6:19-20), so the enemy wants to use human bodies for evil purposes (Rom. 6:12-13). The enemy said, in effect, "Give me your body," to Joseph (Gen. 39) and Daniel (Dan. 1); but they said, "No!" But when the enemy said the same to Samson (Jud. 16), David (2 Sam. 11), and Judas (John 13:27), they said, "Yes!" And what a price they paid!

Abraham did not accept King Bera's offer. Instead, it is likely that Abraham gave everyone he had rescued opportunity to come with him and trust the true and living God. Abraham was a powerful sheik, and his neighbors knew about his tent and his altar. But there is no indication that any of them (including Lot's family) accepted his invitation. Except for Lot and two of his daughters, they all perished in the destruction of Sodom.

A new blessing. Melchizedek had something better to offer Abraham: the blessing of the "Most High God, possessor of heaven and earth." *Abraham lived by the blessing of the Lord, not the bribery of the world.* He did not want anybody to think that the world made him rich. Even a small thing like a shoelace might affect his walk! Too many servants of God have weakened their testimony by accepting applause and gifts from the people of the world. You cannot be a servant of God and a celebrity in the world at the same time.

Melchizedek met Abraham after the battle *to strengthen him for the victory.* The Lord knows the temptations we face after we have defeated the enemy. Abraham had met the Lord *before the battle* and promised to take nothing for himself from the spoils of victory. He was single-minded as he led his army, and God gave him victory.

Abraham did not impose his convictions on his allies— Aner, Eschol, and Mamre (Gen. 14:24). If they wanted to take part of the spoils, that was their business; and he would not criticize them. Nor did he expect them to give tithes to Melchizedek. Abraham was a pilgrim and stranger, while his allies were men of the world whose conduct was governed by a different set of standards. "Others may—you cannot."

Genesis 14:20 is the first mention of tithing in the Bible. To tithe is to give God 10 percent, whether of money, farm produce, or animals. (The Heb. word means "ten.") When we tithe, we acknowledge that God owns everything and that we are grateful stewards of His wealth. The Jews paid an annual tithe to the Lord (Lev. 27:30-33) as well as a tithe every third year especially for the poor (Deut. 26:12-15). They could also tithe the remaining 90 percent for a special "festive offering" to be enjoyed in Jerusalem (Deut. 12:5-19).

The practice of tithing antedated the Law of Moses; for not only did Abraham tithe, but so did Jacob (Gen. 28:22). For this reason, many Christians believe that God's people today should begin their giving with the tithe. A godly deacon said to me once, "If the Old Testament Jew under Law could tithe, how much more ought New Testament Christians under grace!" The New Testament plan for giving is outlined in 2 Corinthians 8–9, but tithing is a good place to start.

We must be careful to give out of the devotion of our hearts, and not as a "bribe" for God's blessings. The late R. G. LeTourneau, well-known Christian manufacturer and philanthropist, used to say, "If you tithe because it pays—it won't pay!"

But Abraham provides us with a good example of giving. *He brought his gifts to Jesus Christ in the person of Melchizedek.* (See Heb. 7:1-10.) We do not give our tithes and offerings to the church, the pastor, or the members of the finance committee. If our giving is a true act of worship, we will give to the Lord; and, for that reason, we want to give our very best (Mal. 1:6-8).

In one of the churches I pastored, we did not take up offerings on Sundays but provided special boxes at the exits before or after the services. A lad visiting church one day asked his friend what the boxes were for, and he told him, "That's where we put our offerings."

The visitor asked, "What happens to the money?"

"I think they give it to Brother Eastep," the boy replied. (Dr. D.B. Eastep was the pastor at that time.)

Even more perplexed, the lad asked, "Well, what does Brother Eastep do with it?"

This time the boy was ready: "I don't know how he does it, *but he gives it to God!*"

When my godly predecessor heard that story, he laughed heartily. He knew (as we all know) that each worshiper must bring his or her gifts to the Lord and give from a grateful heart. All God's people are priests and can bring their sacrifices to Him (1 Peter 2:5, 9).

Abraham was *prompt in his giving*. His stewardship principles were firmly fixed in his heart so there was no reason to delay.

He was also *proportionate in his giving,* a policy encouraged by the Apostle Paul (1 Cor. 16:1-2). Tithing is a good place to begin; but as the Lord blesses, we must increase that percentage if we are to practice the kind of "grace giving" that is described in 2 Corinthians 8–9.

Abraham gave *because he loved God and wanted to acknowledge His greatness and His goodness.* What a contrast between "the Most High God" and the heathen idols! Abraham's God is possessor (Creator) of heaven and earth (Gen. 14:19; see Isa. 40). He deserves all the worship and praise of all of His people!

Before the battle, Abraham lifted his hand by faith in a solemn vow to God that he would take nothing from the spoils. He had a single heart and mind as he led the army (Matt. 6:24).

During the battle, Abraham wielded his sword by faith and trusted God for victory.

After the battle, by faith Abraham closed his hands to the King of Sodom but opened his hands to the King of Salem, receiving bread and wine and giving tithes.

"And this is the victory that has overcome the world—our faith" (1 John 5:4, NKJV).

[Note: You can study more about Melchizedek in *Be Confident,* an exposition of Hebrews; and "grace giving" is explained in *Be Encouraged,* an exposition of 2 Corinthians.]

FOUR

The Dark Night of the Soul

One who truly fears God, and is obedient to Him, may be in a condition of darkness, and have no light; and he may walk many days and years in that condition. . . ."

So wrote the Puritan divine Thomas Goodwin (1600–1679), and the Prophet Isaiah agrees with him: "Who among you fears the Lord? Who obeys the voice of His Servant? Who walks in darkness and has no light? Let him trust in the name of the Lord and rely upon his God" (Isa. 50:10, NKJV).

At times even the most dedicated Christian feels "in the dark" and wonders why God seems so far away. During the Boxer Rebellion, the China Inland Mission suffered greatly; and its founder, J. Hudson Taylor, said to a friend, "I cannot read; I cannot think; I cannot even pray; but I can trust." It was a dark time, but God eventually gave light.

Abraham had an experience of what spiritual directors call "the dark night of the soul." The term comes from a sixteenth-century spiritual classic of that title by St. John of the Cross. Based on the night scenes described in the Song of Songs, the book tells how the child of God enters into deeper love and faith by experiencing temporary darkness and seem-

43

ing separation from God. It is not an easy thing to experience, but sometimes necessary.

Abraham had three great concerns. During that "dark-night" experience, God met all three of them.

1. His safety (Gen. 15:1)

Listening to himself. The previous chapter focused on Abraham's actions, but this chapter deals with his emotions, including the "horror of great darkness" (15:12). People with faith are also people with feelings, and feelings must not be discredited or ignored. Many orthodox Christians are prone to emphasize the mind and will and minimize the emotions, but this is a grave error that can lead to an unbalanced life.

We are made in the image of God, and this includes our emotions. While it is unwise to trust your emotions and bypass your mind, or let your emotions get out of control, it is also unwise to deny and suppress your emotions and become a religious robot. In the Psalms, David and the other writers told God honestly how they felt about Him, themselves, and their circumstances; and this is a good example for us to follow. Jesus was a real man, and He expressed openly His emotions of joy, sorrow, holy anger, and love.

But now that the battle was won, why would Abraham be afraid? For one thing, he was human; and our emotions can "fall apart" after a time of great danger and difficulty. This helps explain why Elijah was so discouraged after the victory over Baal on Mount Carmel (1 Kings 19). After the mountain-top comes the valley.

Another factor was the possibility that the four kings might return with reinforcements and .attack Abraham's camp. Abraham knew that Eastern kings did not take defeat lightly or let enmity die down quickly. And suppose Abraham were killed? What would happen to God's covenant and promise?

Listening to God. You certainly ought to "listen to your

feelings" and be honest about them. "When a person assumes responsibility for his feelings," writes psychiatrist David Viscott, "he assumes responsibility for his world." But don't stop there: Take time to listen to God, and receive His words of encouragement. This is the first time in the Bible you find the phrase "the word of the Lord came"; it is used more than 100 times in the Old Testament. The faith that conquers fear is faith in the Word, not faith in feelings.

God spoke to his friend by name (John 10:3). When I was a lad, I often went shopping for my mother; and the clerks in the stores would call me by name and ask about my family. When my parents went to the bank, the tellers usually knew who they were and greeted them. With very few exceptions, the clerks I meet today see me only as a number in the computer. It seems incredible, but the God who names and numbers all the stars also knows your name and is concerned about your needs (Ps. 147:3-4).

This is also the first time you find the assuring words "fear not" in the Bible. God repeated them to Isaac (Gen. 26:24) and Jacob (46:3) and often to the people of Israel (Ex. 14:13; 20:20; Num. 14:9; Deut. 1:21). The "fear not" promises in Isaiah are good to read and ponder when you find yourself dealing with fear (Isa. 41:10, 13-14; 43:1, 5; 44:2, 8).

God's remedy for Abraham's fear was to remind him who He was: "I am thy shield, and thy exceedingly great reward" (Gen. 15:1). God's I AM is perfectly adequate for man's "I am not." "Be still, and know that I am God" (Ps. 46:10). Your life is only as big as your faith, and your faith is only as big as your God. If you spend all your time looking at yourself, you will get discouraged; but if you look to God by faith, you will be encouraged.

God is our shield and our reward, our protection and our provision. Abraham didn't have to worry about another battle because the Lord would protect him. And he didn't need to regret losing the wealth offered him by the King of Sodom because God would reward him in far greater ways. This is the Old Testament equivalent of Matthew 6:33 and Philippians 4:19.

Protection and *provision* are blessings that the world is seeking and the politicians are promising whenever they run for office. Candidates offer voters protection from war and danger on the streets as well as provision for jobs, health care, education, and old age. Some of the promises are kept, but many of them are forgotten. Almighty God is the only One who can offer you protection and provision and keep His promises. "For the Lord God is a sun and shield; the Lord will give grace and glory. No good thing will He withhold from them that walk uprightly" (Ps. 84:11).

2. His heir (Gen. 15:2-6)

Asking (Gen. 15:2-3). God had promised Abraham that his descendants would be as numerous as the dust of the earth (13:16) and that they would bring blessing to the whole world (12:1-3). But Abraham and Sarah were still childless; and if Abraham died, the only heir he had was his "chief of staff" — Eliezer. (He may be the servant mentioned in 24:2.) Lot was no longer in the picture, and Abraham's other relatives were 500 miles away in Mesopotamia. What had happened to the promise?

Abraham's concern was not just for himself and his wife, though like all Eastern couples, they wanted children. His concern was for the working out of God's plan of salvation for the whole world. God had a glorious plan, and God made a gracious promise, *but God seemed to be doing nothing!* Abraham and Sarah were getting older, and time was running out.

One of the basic lessons in "the school of faith" is: *God's will must be fulfilled in God's way and in God's time.* God did not expect Abraham and Sarah to figure out how to have an heir; all He asked was that they be available so He could accomplish His purposes in and through them. What Abraham and Sarah did not realize was that God was waiting for them to be "as good as dead" so that God alone would receive the power and glory.

It is good to share your concerns with the Lord, even if what you say seems to evidence unbelief or impatience in your heart. God is not deaf to your questions or unconcerned about your feelings. He did not rebuke Abraham; instead, He gave him the assurances that he needed. "Casting all your care upon Him, for He careth for you" (1 Peter 5:7).

Looking (Gen. 15:4-5). God made it clear that Abraham *alone* would be the father of the future heir. *Heirship depends on sonship* (Rom. 8:14-17). Then God dramatically assured Abraham that this one heir would be the father of so many descendants that nobody would be able to count them. *Even when life is dark, you can still see the stars.* Someone has well said, "When the outlook is bleak, try the uplook." Abraham had been looking *around,* trying to solve his problem; but the answer lay in looking *up.*

About 30,000 stars are listed in the General Catalog used by astronomers, but it is estimated that there are 100 billion more! God did not say that Abraham would have that many descendants but that, like the stars, there would be too many to count. Whether Abraham looked *down* at the dust (Gen. 13:14) or *up* at the stars (15:5), he would recall God's promise and have confidence. This promise was repeated to Abraham (22:17) and reaffirmed to Isaac (26:4).

Believing (Gen. 15:6). Promises do us no good unless we believe them and act on them. Abraham had already trusted God's promise (12:1-3) and proved it by leaving home and going to Canaan (Heb. 11:8). But Genesis 15:6 is the first reference in the Bible to Abraham's faith. It is the John 3:16 of the Old Testament; and for this reason, the New Testament writers use it to illustrate salvation by faith.

There are only five words in the Hebrew original of Genesis 15:6, but what a wealth of meaning they contain. The verse is quoted three times in the New Testament: Galatians 3:6; Romans 4:3; and James 2:23. The three key words are *believe*, *counted*, and *righteousness*.

Abraham *believed* God, which is literally, "Abraham said, 'Amen, God!' " The Hebrew word translated "believed" means "to lean your whole weight upon." Abraham leaned wholly on the promise of God and the God of the promise. We are not saved by *making promises* to God but by *believing the promises* of God. In the Gospel of John, which was written to tell people how to be saved (John 20:31), the word "believe" is used nearly 100 times. Salvation is the gracious gift of God, and it is received by faith (Eph. 2:8-9).

What was Abraham's greatest need? *Righteousness.* This is the greatest need of people in our world today, for "all have sinned, and come short of the glory of God" (Rom. 3:23). "There is none righteous, no, not one" (3:10). It is not enough to be "religious"; God demands that we have perfect righteousness or He will not let us enter His heaven.

How did Abraham receive this righteousness? He believed the Lord, and righteousness was *imputed* to him. "Impute" means "to put to one's account." On the cross, our sins were put on Jesus' account ("numbered [counted] with the transgressors," Isa. 53:12) when He suffered the punishment that belonged to us (53:6). When you trust Him, His righteousness is put on your account (2 Cor. 5:21), and you stand righteous and forgiven before a holy God.

Abraham proved his faith by his works when he offered Isaac on the altar (James 2:14-24). Abraham was not saved by obeying God, or even promising to obey God; but his obedience proved his faith. Sinners are not saved by faith plus works but by a faith that works.

Take time to read Galatians 3, Romans 4, and James 2; and you will see how Abraham illustrates salvation by faith. In Galatians 3, Paul focuses on *believe;* in Romans 4, he deals with *impute;* and in James 2, James explains *righteousness.* It takes three New Testament chapters to unfold one verse!

The answer to Abraham's fear was God's presence—I AM. The answer to Abraham's concern about his heir was God's promise—I WILL. How will God answer Abraham's third concern?

3. His land (Gen. 15:7-21)

Affirmation (Gen. 15:7). God had told Abraham that He would give the land of Canaan to him and his descendants (12:7; 13:15, 17), and now He reaffirmed that promise. The land is an important part of the covenant for it is in the land of Israel that the divine drama of "salvation history" was enacted. The land of Israel will also be the stage for the final act of that drama when the Messiah returns to reign on earth.

For centuries, Israel was a nation without a land; and it seemed that the covenant promises would not be fulfilled. In 1932, British expositor G. Campbell Morgan wrote, "I am now quite convinced that the teaching of Scripture as a whole is that there is no future for Israel as an earthly people at all" (*This Was His Faith,* p. 290). Then came May 14, 1948, and the rebirth of national Israel! Just as God kept His promise to Abraham and sent the Messiah, so He will keep His promise and restore the land to His people.

Assurance (Gen. 15:8-12). Abraham's question was not a sign of unbelief but a request for a token of assurance. He was confident that God would give him the promised son, but the land was in the hands of ten pagan nations (15:19-21). It was one thing for Abraham to *own* the land, but how would his descendants *possess* it so they could *enjoy* it?

What is described in 15:9-17 was known in that day as

"cutting a covenant." This solemn ritual involved the death of animals and the binding of people to a promise. The persons making the covenant would sacrifice several animals and divide the bodies, placing the halves opposite each other on the ground. Then the parties would walk between the pieces of the sacrifices in declaration that, if they failed to keep their word, they deserved the same fate as the animals. (See Jer. 34:18-19.)

But Abraham's experience was different. He killed the animals, laid them on the ground, and spent the rest of the day fighting off the birds of prey that were attracted to the flesh and blood. When the sun went down, Abraham fell into a deep sleep; and then God appeared to him and spoke to him. *But God alone passed between the parts of the sacrifices!* (Gen. 15:17) It was God who made promises to Abraham, not Abraham who made promises to God. There were no conditions attached; the covenant of grace came from the generous heart of God.

Anticipation (Gen. 15:13-21). Out of the "horror of great darkness," Abraham heard the terms of God's covenant and discovered God's plan for the nation (15:13-14, 16-17), himself (15:15), and the land (15:18-21).

The nation (Gen. 15:13-14, 16-17). Jacob and his family went to Egypt to be protected by Joseph, and there they grew into a mighty people (Gen. 46–Ex. 1). Arriving in Egypt as honored guests, the Jews eventually became a threat; so Pharaoh made them slaves and afflicted them greatly (Ex. 1:11-12). Perhaps the smoking furnace (Gen. 15:17) was a symbol of the nation's suffering in Egypt (Deut. 4:20). Pharaoh's cruelty could not exterminate the nation because God had plans for His chosen people. God judged Egypt with ten plagues and then enabled Moses to lead the people out triumphantly (Ex. 5–15).

The events and their timing were in the hands of God. The

400 years of Genesis 15:13 refers to Israel's entire stay in Egypt, from Jacob's arrival to the Exodus. It is a round figure, because Exodus 12:40 puts it at 430 years. (See also Acts 7:6.) Why did God wait so long to deliver His people? Because God was long-suffering with the nations in Canaan and delayed their judgment so they might have more time to repent (2 Peter 3:8-9; Matt. 23:32). Those who condemn Israel (and God) for the way the Canaanites were treated seem to forget that God gave them centuries to repent of their wickedness.

Abraham (Gen. 15:15). Abraham's "good old age" was 175 years (Gen. 25:7), which means he walked with God for a century (12:4). In spite of Abraham's occasional failures, he accomplished the will of God and brought blessing to the whole world. This promise from God must have given Abraham and Sarah great encouragement during times of difficulty, just as promises like Philippians 1:6 and Ephesians 2:10 encourage God's people today.

The land (Gen. 15:18-21). At the beginning of Abraham's pilgrimage, God said to him, "I will show thee" the land (12:1). Later He said, "I will give it unto thee" (13:15-17). But now His word is, "To your descendants I have given this land" (15:18, NASB). God's covenant made it a settled matter: The land belongs to Abraham's descendants through Isaac.

Solomon exercised dominion over a vast area (1 Kings 4:21; Ps. 72:8), but Israel did not *possess* all that land. The kings merely acknowledged Solomon's sovereignty and paid tribute to him. When Jesus Christ reigns from the throne of David (Matt. 19:28; Luke 1:32), the land of Israel will reach the full dimensions promised by God.

God's covenant with Abraham stands no matter what Israel believes. The covenant is unconditional; its fulfillment does not depend on man's faith or faithfulness. In like manner, the New Covenant established by Jesus Christ is dependable whether people accept it or not. Those who put their faith in Jesus Christ enter into that covenant and receive eternal salvation (Heb. 5:9; 9:12), an eternal inheritance (9:15), and eternal glory (1 Peter 5:10).

When Abraham was concerned about himself, God assured him by saying, "I AM!" When he was concerned about his heir, he heard God say, "I will!" His concern about the land was met by God's, "I have given!"

In Jesus Christ, God gives those same assurances to His people today.

Abraham believed God.

Do you believe?

[For a more detailed study of Galatians 3, see *Be Free*. Romans 4 is explained in *Be Right*. The subject of faith and works in James 2 is dealt with in *Be Mature*. These titles are published by Victor Books.]

FIVE

Beware of Detours!

Back in the '60s, my wife and I enjoyed a brief vacation in the beautiful foothills of the Appalachian Mountains. As we began to drive home, she said, "Let's take this side road. It looks interesting."

Interesting! It turned out to be one of the worst rural roads we have ever encountered, including some we've seen on mission fields overseas. There were no potholes; they were all craters. And while my car was raising dust, my impatience was raising my temper. As we carefully rounded a curve, we concluded that few people ever took this route; for there in front of us were two turtles, leisurely taking a walk in one of the two ruts that kept you on the road.

When we finally reached civilization and a paved road, I thought of the statement Vance Havner often made: "The detour is always worse than the main road."

Genesis 16 records a painful detour that Abraham and Sarah made in their pilgrim walk, a detour that brought conflict not only into their home but also into the world. What today's journalists call "the Arab-Israeli conflict" began right here.

But this account is much more than ancient history with modern consequences. It's a good lesson for God's people about walking by faith and waiting for God to fulfill His promises in His way and in His time. As you study the stages in the experience of Abraham and Sarah, you will see how dangerous it is to depend on your own wisdom.

1. Waiting (Gen. 16:1a)

Abraham was now eighty-five years old. He had been walking with the Lord for ten years and had learned some valuable lessons about faith. God had promised Abraham and Sarah a child but had not told them when the child would be born. It was a period of waiting, and most people don't like to wait. But it is through "faith and patience [that we] inherit the promises" (Heb. 6:12).

God has a perfect timetable for all that He wants to do. After all, this event was not the birth of just another baby: It was part of God's great plan of salvation for the whole world. However, as Sarah waited for something to happen, she became impatient.

Why did God wait so long? He wanted Abraham and Sarah to be physically "as good as dead" (Heb. 11:12) so that God alone would get the glory. At age eighty-five, Abraham was still virile enough to father a child by Hagar; so the time for the miracle baby had not yet arrived. Whatever is truly done by faith is done *for the glory of God* (Rom. 4:20) and not for the praise of man.

A willingness to wait on the Lord is another evidence that you are walking by faith. "He that believeth shall not make haste" (Isa. 28:16). Paul quoted this verse in Romans 10:11 and amplified its meaning: "Whosoever believeth on Him shall not be ashamed." (The same Holy Spirit inspired both Isaiah and Paul, and He has the right to make these changes.) Whenever we stop trusting God, we start to "make haste" in the wrong direction and we end up being ashamed.

A third evidence of faith is *that you are acting on the author-*

ity of God's Word. "So, then, faith cometh by hearing, and hearing by the Word of God" (Rom. 10:17). You can act by faith, and know that God will bless, if you are obeying what He says in His Word. Hebrews 11 records the mighty acts of ordinary men and women who dared to believe God's promises and obey His commandments.

Finally, whenever you act by faith, *God will give joy and peace in your life.* "Now the God of hope fill you with all joy and peace in believing" (Rom. 15:13). Conflict may surround you, but you will have God's peace and joy within you.

These, then, are the evidences of true biblical faith: (1) you are willing to wait; (2) you are concerned only for the glory of God; (3) you are obeying God's Word; and (4) you have God's joy and peace within. While Abraham and Sarah were waiting, God was increasing their faith and patience and building character (James 1:1-4). Then something happened that put Abraham and Sarah on a painful detour.

2. Scheming (Gen. 16:1b-4a)

Sarah knew that she was incapable of bearing a child but that her husband was still capable of begetting a child. God had specifically named Abraham as the father of the promised heir, *but He had not yet identified the mother.* Logically, it would be Abraham's wife; but perhaps God had other plans. Sarah was "second-guessing" God, and this is a dangerous thing to do. Remember, true faith is based on the Word of God (Rom. 10:17) and not on the wisdom of man (Prov. 3:5-6), because "faith is living without scheming." Sarah said, "It may be"; she did not say, "Thus saith the Lord!" God had told Abraham, "Know of a surety" (Gen. 15:13); but Sarah had no such assurance on which to base her actions.

Furthermore, Sarah was not concerned about the glory of God; her only goal was "that I may obtain children by her" (16:2). Perhaps there is a hint of disappointment with God and even *blaming* God when she says, "The Lord hath restrained me from bearing" (16:2). It has often been said that God's delays are not God's denials, but Satan whispers to us, "God is holding out on you! If He loved you, things would be different! Blame Him!" (See 3:1-6.)

Abraham's taking Hagar as a second wife was perfectly legal according to the marriage code of that day. In later years, Jacob would marry his wives' maids, Bilhah and Zilpah; and each would give him two sons. Moreover, the plan seemed to be successful, for Hagar conceived a child. Perhaps Sarah was right after all.

But not everything that is legal or that appears to be successful is approved by the will of God. God never accepted Hagar as Abraham's wife; the Angel of the Lord called her "Sarah's maid" (16:8). Later she was called "this bondwoman and her son" (21:10), not "Abraham's wife and son." Why? Because "whatever is not of faith is sin" (Rom. 14:23). God rejected the whole enterprise because He had something far better in mind for Abraham and Sarah.

When you review the four evidences of biblical faith that were explained above, you can see that Abraham and Sarah did not pass the test. They were unwilling to wait on the Lord but rushed ahead with their own plans. They acted only to please themselves and not to glorify God. They were not obeying the Word, and what they did certainly did not bring joy and peace to their hearts or their home.

Scottish novelist George MacDonald was right when he said, "In whatever man does without God, he must fail miserably, or succeed more miserably." This leads us to the third stage in Abraham and Sarah's "detour" experience.

3. Fighting (Gen. 16:4b-6)

When you follow the wisdom of the world, you will end up warring like the world (James 3:13-18). Of all fights, family fights are the most painful and the most difficult to settle. Had Hagar maintained the attitude of a servant, things might have been different; but she became proud, and this irritated her mistress (Prov. 30:21-23).

"Having begun in the Spirit, are ye now made perfect by the flesh?" Paul asked (Gal. 3:3); and you see this illustrated in Abraham's home. He and Sarah had begun in the Spirit when they put their faith in the Lord, but now they had turned to the flesh for help; and some of the works of the flesh were starting to appear (Gal. 5:19-21). Abraham, Sarah, and Hagar were at war with each other because they were at war with the Lord, and they were at war with the Lord because they had selfish desires warring within their own hearts (James 4:1-10).

The first thing they should have done was build an altar, worship the Lord, and tell Him their problems. They should have confessed their sins and received His gracious forgiveness. Once you stop fighting with God and with yourself, you will have an easier time not fighting with others. The first step toward reconciliation with others is getting right with God.

However, instead of facing their sins honestly, each of the persons involved took a different course; and this only made things worse. Sarah's solution was *to blame her husband* and *mistreat her servant* as she gave vent to her anger. She seems to have forgotten that she was the one who had made the marriage suggestion in the first place. Abraham's solution was to give in to his wife and *abdicate spiritual headship* in the home. He should have had pity for a helpless servant who was pregnant, but he allowed Sarah to mistreat her. He should have summoned them all to the altar, but he did not.

Hagar's solution was to *run away from the problem,* a tactic we all learned from Adam and Eve (Gen. 3:8). However, you soon discover that you cannot solve problems by running away. Abraham learned that when he fled to Egypt (12:10ff). There was peace in the home for a short time, but it was not the "peace of God." It was only a brittle, temporary truce that soon would fail.

4. Submitting (Gen. 16:7-16)

James 4:1-10 explains why Christians fight and how Christians can be at peace. Our battles among ourselves are caused because we obey our three enemies: the world (James 4:4), the flesh (4:1), and the devil (4:7). How can we expect to be at peace with God and each other if we are living for the enemy! "God resists the proud, but gives grace to the humble. Therefore submit to God" (4:6-7, NKJV).

Hagar had to submit to God (Gen. 16:7-14). This is the first appearance in Scripture of the Angel of the Lord, who is generally identified as our Lord Jesus Christ. In Genesis 16:10, the angel promised to do what only God can do; and in 16:13, Hagar called the angel "God." These pre-Incarnation visits of Jesus Christ to the earth were to meet special needs and to accomplish special tasks. The fact that the Son of God took on a temporary body, left heaven, and came down to help a rejected servant-girl surely reveals His grace and love. His servants Abraham and Sarah had sinned against the Lord and against Hagar, but the Lord did not desert them.

The angel called her "Sarah's maid," which suggests that God did not accept her marriage to Abraham. Apparently Hagar was on her way back to Egypt when she met the angel, but God told her to return to Abraham's camp and submit herself to her mistress. That would take a great deal of faith, because Sarah had mistreated Hagar before and might do it again.

God then told her that she was pregnant with a son whom she should name Ishmael ("God hears"). While he would not be Abraham's heir in the blessings of the covenant, Ishmael would still enjoy blessings from God since he was Abraham's son. God promised to multiply Ishmael's descendants and make them into great nations (21:18; 25:12-18), and He did; for Ishmael is the founder of the Arab peoples.

Ishmael would be a "wild donkey of a man" (16:12, NIV), which is not a very flattering description. It identified him with the wilderness where he lived by his skill as an archer (Gen. 21:20-21; Job 24:5). It also revealed his independent and pugnacious nature.

He would be a hated man, living "in hostility toward all his brothers" (Gen. 16:12, NIV). While we must not apply these traits to *every* descendant of Ishmael, the centuries-long hostility between the Jews and the Arabs is too well known to be ignored. The Arab nations are independent peoples, dwelling in the desert lands and resisting the encroachments of other nations, especially Israel and her allies.

Hagar's wilderness experience brought her face-to-face with God and taught her some important truths about Him. She learned that He is the living God who sees us and hears our cries when we hurt. The name of the well means "The well of One who lives and sees me." He is a personal God, concerned about abused people and unborn babies. He knows the future and cares for those who will trust Him.

Hagar did return and submit herself to Sarah. Surely she apologized for being arrogant, for despising her mistress, and for running away. She trusted God to protect her and her son and to care for them in the years to come. We never solve life's problems by running away. Submit to God and trust Him to work things out for your good and His glory.

Sarah had to submit to God. How did Sarah feel when Hagar came back to the camp and reported that God had talked with her? Did God have time for a poor servant? Was God concerned about a slave-girl's baby? Did the God of Israel care for an Egyptian? Yes, because that Egyptian's baby had Abraham as a father; and God had a covenant with Abraham. The record does not tell us how Sarah responded, but it would appear that she accepted both Hagar and her report and took her back as her servant. Sarah did not mistreat her again; for, after all, God was watching!

Abraham had to submit to God. In this entire episode, Abraham played a rather passive role. He let Sarah talk him into marrying Hagar, and he allowed Sarah to mistreat Hagar and drive her from the camp. Apparently, Abraham did not offer to help Hagar in any way. (Later, he made up for that—Gen. 21:9ff.) But when his son was born, Abraham acknowledged him and obediently gave him the name that God had appointed.

Both Abraham and Sarah had to learn to live with their mistakes. Certainly Abraham enjoyed watching the boy grow up, and the old man's heart was full of love for him (17:18). But Abraham knew that Ishmael would not be a permanent part of the covenant family. God's solution to the "Ishmael problem" was not to blame Abraham, Sarah, or Hagar, but *to send another baby into the home—Isaac.* Ishmael did not give Abraham and Sarah any trouble *until Isaac came along;* then he started to create problems (21:1-11). As we shall see in later chapters, all of these things have profound theological significance for the Christian believer today.

As you review the chapter, you will see that several key texts from Romans are illustrated by what is recorded here.

"For whatsoever is not of faith is sin" (Rom. 14:23). Be sure that your plans and procedures can pass the four "tests of faith" outlined above. People may agree with you, and the law may defend you; but if God cannot bless you, *don't do it!* Let God accomplish His will in His way and in His time. Sarah tried to run ahead of God, and she created problems that are with us yet today.

"They who receive abundance of grace and of the gift of righ-

teousness shall reign in life" (Rom. 5:17). In Genesis 15, grace was reigning through righteousness because of Abraham's faith (15:6); and Abraham was reigning in life to the glory of God. But he abdicated the throne in chapter 16, and sin started to reign. Unbelief, impatience, anger, pride, and indifference took over in Abraham's home and almost destroyed it. God's people are kings and priests (Rev. 1:6), who should "reign in life" by yielding to Jesus Christ (see Rom. 6:11-14).

"But where sin abounded, grace did much more abound" (Rom. 5:20). This does not mean that God winks at sin or that abundant sinning is the key to abundant grace (6:1-7). Rather, it means that God's grace is greater than man's sin and can accomplish God's best even when men do their worst. In grace, God saw Hagar fleeing to Egypt; and He came to her and met her needs. He made her the mother of a great nation. Of course, He did it because of Abraham; but God's covenant with Abraham was a covenant of grace.

From the human viewpoint, this "detour" was a tragedy that brought God's great salvation plan to a standstill. Consider, however, the divine point of view. God is never caught by surprise. When He cannot rule, He overrules; and He always accomplishes His purposes.

Satan wants us to think that our "disobedience detours" must become the permanent road for the rest of our lives; *but this is a lie.* Like Abraham and Sarah, we can confess our sins, accept God's cleansing (1 John 1:9), and then learn to live with our mistakes. Yes, there will be pain and regret; but God's grace will overcome in the end.

George Morrison is worth quoting again: "The victorious Christian life is a series of new beginnings."

S I X

What's in a Name?

At some point in your education, you may have read Shakespeare's *Romeo and Juliet;* and you discovered in act 2 that famous quotation: "What's in a name? That which we call a rose by any other word would smell as sweet."

Juliet spoke those words as she talked to herself on her balcony, ignorant of the fact that Romeo was listening below. She was pondering the fact that she belonged to the Capulet family and he to the rival Montagues, and that this accident of birth hindered them from getting married. What difference did two names make? No matter what his name was, Romeo was still her love!

Shakespeare notwithstanding, if you had asked a biblical character the question, "What's in a name?" that person would have replied: "Everything! Our names are very important!" Names might record something significant about one's birth (Gen. 29:31–30:24) or about some life-changing experience. Jacob was renamed Israel after a night of wrestling with God (32:24-32), and Simon received the name Peter (rock) when he met Jesus Christ (John 1:40-42). The names assigned to unborn babies even carried messages (Gen. 16:11; Matt. 1:18-25).

In this chapter, you will discover four new names and a name that will always be old because it cannot be changed.

1. God Almighty (Gen. 17:1-2)

Revelation. The Hebrew name is "El Shaddai" (shuh-DYE), and this is the first time it occurs in Scripture. "Shaddai" is translated as "Almighty" forty-eight times in the Old Testament. In the New Testament, the Greek equivalent is used in 2 Corinthians 6:18 and Revelation 1:8; 4:8; 11:17; 15:3; 16:7 and 14; 19:6 and 15; and 21:22. It is translated "Almighty" except in Revelation 19:6 ("omnipotent").

"El" is the name of God that speaks of power; but what does "Shaddai" mean? Scholars do not agree. Some say it comes from a Hebrew word meaning "to be strong"; others prefer a word meaning "mountain" or "breast." Metaphorically, a mountain is a "breast" that rises up from the plain; and certainly a mountain is a symbol of strength. If we combine these several ideas, we might say that "El Shaddai" is the name of "the all-powerful and all-sufficient God who can do anything and meet any need."

But why would God reveal this name to Abraham at this time, at the close of thirteen years of silence? *Because God was going to tell His friend that Sarah would have a son.* The Lord wanted Abraham to know that He is the God who is all-sufficient and all-powerful, and that nothing is too hard for Him. God says "I will" twelve times in this chapter; He is about to do the miraculous.

After Abraham's battle with the four kings, God came to him as a warrior and told him He was his "shield." When Abraham wondered about his refusal of Sodom's wealth, God told him He was his "exceedingly great reward" (Gen. 15:1). Now when Abraham and Sarah were "as good as dead," God assured them that He was more than sufficient to bring about the miracle birth. God comes to us in the ways we need Him most.

Responsibility. Revelation always brings responsibility. Enoch and Noah had walked *with* God (5:22; 6:8-9), but Abraham was to walk *before* God, that is, live in the knowledge that the eyes of God were always upon him (Heb. 4:13). The word "perfect" does not mean "sinless," for that would be an impossible goal for anyone to reach (1 Kings 8:46). The word means "single-hearted, without blame, sincere, wholly devoted to the Lord." In Exodus 12:5, the word refers to a "perfect" sacrifice without blemish. It was a call for integrity.

This is not to suggest that God's people should settle for anything less than striving to conform to His will. "His desire for us should be our aim and desire for ourselves," wrote Alexander Maclaren. "It is more blessed to be smitten with the longing to win the unwon than to stagnate in ignoble contentment with partial attainments. Better to climb, with faces turned upwards to the inaccessible peak, than to lie at ease in the fat valleys" (*Expositions of Holy Scripture*, vol. 1, p. 120 [Baker Book House, 1974]).

The secret of a perfect walk before God is a personal worship of God. Like Abraham, every believer must fall before the Lord and yield everything to Him. If He is "El Shaddai—God Almighty," then who are we to resist His will?

Relationship. The phrase "My covenant" is used nine times in this chapter and defines God's relationship with Abraham. This was not another covenant, different from the one God had already established with Abraham (Gen. 12:1-3; 15:1-21). It was a reaffirmation of that covenant, with the important addition of circumcision, the sign and seal of the covenant.

God promised once again to multiply Abraham's family, even though he and his wife did not have any children. His descendants would be "as the dust of the earth" (13:16) and as the stars of the heavens (15:5). These two comparisons—earth and heaven—suggest that Abraham would have a physical family, the Jews (Matt. 3:9), and a spiritual family made up of all who believe in Jesus Christ (Gal. 3:26-29).

2. Abraham (Gen. 17:3-14, 23-27)

The people. "Abram" means "exalted father"; "Abraham" means "father of a multitude." When Abraham informed the people in his camp that he had a new name, some of them must have smiled and said, "Father of a multitude! Why, he and his wife are too old to have children!" Whether he looked beneath his feet or up into the heavens, or whenever anyone called him by name, Abraham was reminded of God's gracious promise to give him many descendants.

Keep in mind that Abraham's descendants include not only the Jewish people, but also the Arab world (through Ishmael) and the nations listed in Genesis 25:1-4. All who trust Jesus Christ as Savior are spiritual children of Abraham (Gal. 3:6-9), and that will be a vast multitude (Rev. 7:9).

In being fruitful for God, we have nothing in ourselves that will accomplish the task. Abraham and Sarah had tried their own plan, and it failed miserably. Jesus said, "Without Me, ye can do nothing" (John 15:5). "We say that we depend on the Holy Spirit," wrote Vance Havner, "but actually we are so wired up with our own devices that if the fire does not fall from heaven, we can turn on a switch and produce false fire of our own."

I read about a young Scottish minister who walked proudly into the pulpit to preach his first sermon. He had a brilliant mind and a good education and was confident of himself as he faced his first congregation. But the longer he preached, the more conscious everyone was that "the Lord was not in the wind." He finished his message quickly and came down from the pulpit with his head bowed, his pride now gone. Afterward, one of the members said to him, "If you had gone into the pulpit the way you came down, you might have come down from the pulpit the way you went up."

The land. God's everlasting covenant also included an ever-lasting possession: the land of Canaan. This land is a battle-ground today and always will be until the Lord returns to reign. But as far as God's covenant is concerned, the land belongs to Israel.

The Jews' *ownership* of the land depends solely on God's gracious covenant with Abraham: God gave them the land. But their *possession* and *enjoyment* of the land depends on their faithfulness to obey the Lord. This was the theme of Moses' messages in Deuteronomy. More than sixty times in that book, Moses told the people they would inherit or pos-sess the land; and at least twenty-five times, Moses reminded them that the land was a gift from the Lord. God's name was there (Deut. 12:5, 11, 21), and He would watch over the land to bless it, if His people walked in His ways.

The only piece of ground all the patriarchs possessed was the cave Abraham purchased from Ephron, the son of Zohar, to become a family burial place (Gen. 23; 49:29-31). Jacob and his family had to leave the land and go to Egypt (Gen. 46), but God had promised that they would return to Canaan at the appointed time (15:13-17).

Joshua led them into their land where they conquered the inhabitants and claimed their inheritance. But the people did not stay true to the covenant, so God had to discipline them *in the land* (Jud. 2:10-23). He raised up enemy nations to defeat Israel and put her in bondage. Israel was *in* the land, but she did not *control* it or *enjoy* it (Deut. 28:15ff).

During the reigns of David and Solomon, the people en-joyed their inheritance and served the Lord faithfully. But after the kingdom divided, Israel and Judah both decayed spir-itually (except for occasional interludes of revival) and ended up in bondage: Assyria defeated Israel, and Babylon con-quered Judah. It was then that God disciplined His people *outside their land.* It was as though He were saying, "You have polluted My land with your idols, so I will put you in a land that is addicted to idols. Get your fill of it! After you have been away from your land for seventy years, maybe you will learn to appreciate what I gave you."

God permitted a remnant to return to the land, rebuild the city and the temple, and restore the nation; but it never became a great power again. However, whether Israel is faithful or faithless, the land belongs to her; and one day she will inherit it and enjoy it to the glory of God. Israel's title deed to the land is a vital part of God's everlasting covenant with Abraham.

The sign. In Genesis 17:4, God said, "As for Me"; but in 17:9, He said, "As for you" (NKJV, NASB, NIV). Abraham's part in the covenant was to obey God and mark each male in his house with the sign of the covenant. Circumcision was not a new rite, for other nations practiced it in Abraham's time; but God now gave it new importance and special meaning. For the descendants of Abraham, circumcision was not an option; it was an obligation.

It is important to note that circumcision was not a "sacrament." The performing of it did not convey spiritual blessing to the recipient. An eight-day-old baby boy (Lev. 12:3) would not even understand what was going on; and when he got older, the ritual would have to be explained to him. It was the obedience of the parents that was important; for if they did not obey God in this matter, their son would be cut off from his people (Gen. 17:14). The covenant people must bear the mark of the covenant.

Since God's covenant involved Abraham's "seed," it was fitting that the mark of the covenant be on the male organ of generation. Since all people are conceived in sin (Ps. 51:5), this special mark would remind them that they were accepted by God because of His gracious covenant. It was God who chose the Jews, not the Jews who chose God (Deut. 7:1-11);

and He chose them to be a holy people. Immorality was rampant among the Canaanite peoples, and was even a part of their religion; but the people of Israel were "marked" to be separate from the evil around them.

Unfortunately, the Jewish people eventually made this ritual a means of salvation. Circumcision was a guarantee that you were accepted by God. (Some people today place the same false confidence in baptism, Communion, and other religious rites that can be very meaningful if rightly used.) *They did not realize that circumcision stood for something much deeper: the person's relationship to God.* God wants us to "circumcise our hearts" and be totally devoted to Him in love and obedience (Deut. 10:16; 30:6; Jer. 4:4; Rom. 2:28-29).

Romans 4:9-12 makes it clear that the physical operation had nothing to do with Abraham's eternal salvation. Abraham had believed God and received God's righteousness *before he ever was circumcised* (Gen. 15:6). Circumcision was not the *means* of his salvation but the *mark* of his separation as a man in covenant relationship with God. The legalistic element in the early church tried to make circumcision and obedience to the Law a requirement for salvation for the Gentiles, but this heresy was refuted (Acts 15:1-35). In his Galatian Epistle, Paul argues convincingly for salvation by grace alone.

What does all of this mean to Christian believers today? The seal of our salvation is not an external rite but the presence of an internal witness in the person of the Holy Spirit of God (Eph. 1:13; 4:30; Rom. 8:9, 16). We have experienced a "spiritual circumcision" (Col. 2:9-12) that makes us part of the "true circumcision" (Phil. 3:1-3). When we trusted Christ to save us, the Spirit of God performed "spiritual surgery" that enables us to have victory over the desires of the old nature and the old life. Circumcision removes only a part of the body, but the true "spiritual circumcision" puts off "the body of the sins of the flesh" (Col. 2:11) and deals radically with the sin nature.

This "spiritual circumcision" is accomplished at conversion when the sinner believes in Christ and is baptized by the Spirit into the body of Christ (1 Cor. 12:13). This baptism identifies the believer with Christ in His death, burial, resurrection, and ascension, and also in His circumcision (Col. 2:11-12; Luke 2:21). It is not "the circumcision of Moses" but "the circumcision of Christ" that is important to the Christian believer.

Donald Grey Barnhouse has said, "We have a nature of sin that must be dealt with by the knife. . . . The thing must be dealt with as a whole, and not piecemeal." In Christ, we can "walk in the Spirit and . . . not fulfill the lusts of the flesh" (Gal. 5:16).

Abraham immediately obeyed God and gave every male in his household the mark of the covenant. No doubt when he told them his new name, he also explained what this ritual meant.

3. Sarah (Gen. 17:15-17)

The third new name was "Sarah," which means "princess." (We are not certain what "Sarai" means. Some say "to mock" or "to be contentious." It could also be another form of the word "princess.") Since she would become the mother of kings, it was only right that she be called a princess!

We must not minimize the place of Sarah in God's great plan of salvation. Like her husband (and all of us), she had her faults; but also like her husband, she trusted God and accomplished His purposes (Heb. 11:11). She is not only the mother of the Jewish nation (Isa. 51:2) but also a good example for Christian wives to follow (1 Peter 3:1-6). The Christian husband should treat his wife like a princess, because that is what she is in the Lord.

Three different occasions of laughter are associated with Isaac's birth: Abraham laughed for joy when he heard his wife would give birth to the promised son (Gen. 17:17); Sarah laughed in unbelief when she heard the news (18:9-15); and Sarah laughed for joy when the boy was born (21:6-7). The name Isaac means "he laughs."

Motherhood should be highly esteemed, and the birth of a baby welcomed with joy. While God does not call all women to marry, or all married women to bear children, He does have a special concern for both mothers and children (Pss. 113:9; 127:3-5; Matt. 19:14). In a selfish society, too many people see motherhood as a barrier and children as a burden. In fact, some people consider children such a burden that they destroy them before they have an opportunity to become a blessing.

The womb of the mother is a holy of holies where God is at work (Ps. 139:13-18). How tragic that we turn that womb into a tomb, that holy of holies into a holocaust.

4. Isaac (Gen. 17:18-22)

The first baby in the Bible who was named before birth was Ishmael (16:11), and the second was Isaac. As we shall see when we study Genesis 21, these two boys represent two different births: (1) Ishmael, our first birth after the flesh, and (2) Isaac, our second birth through the Spirit. (See John 3:1-8 and Gal. 4:21-31, especially vv. 28-29.)

From the human point of view, we can understand why Abraham interceded for Ishmael. Ishmael was his son, and the father loved him dearly. They had been together now for thirteen years, and Ishmael was entering adulthood. Was God going to waste all that Abraham had invested in Ishmael? Was there to be no future for the lad? After all, it wasn't Ishmael's fault that he was born! It was Abraham and Sarah who sinned, not the boy.

But from the spiritual point of view, Ishmael could not replace Isaac or even be equal to him in the covenant plan of

God. God had already promised to bless Ishmael (Gen. 16:11), and He kept His promise (25:12-16); but the covenant blessings were not a part of Ishmael's heritage. Isaac alone was to be the heir of all things (25:5-6; Rom. 9:6-13).

There is a practical lesson here for all who seek to live by faith: *When God is preparing a bright future for you, don't cling to the things of the past.* Ishmael represented the past, Isaac the future. Ishmael symbolized man's fleshly way of accomplishing something for God; but Isaac was a miracle baby, born by the power of God. Ishmael brought dissension into the home, but Isaac brought laughter. If you have an "Ishmael" in your life, yield it up to God. God has a perfect plan, and what He plans is the best. It may pain you to give up your cherished dreams, but God's way is always the right way.

Amy Carmichael, missionary to India, wrote to a friend who was perplexed about a painful experience, "I will say what our Heavenly Father said to me long ago, and says to me still very often: 'See in it a chance to die.' "

Perhaps we all need to pray, "Oh, that Ishmael might *die* within me!"

Ishmael did not get a new name, because he represents the flesh; and the flesh cannot be changed. "That which is born of the flesh is flesh" (John 3:6) *and always will be flesh.* "For I know that in me (that is, in my flesh) dwelleth no good thing" (Rom. 7:18). "It is the Spirit who gives life; the flesh profits nothing" (John 6:63, NKJV). The old nature can be disciplined, subdued, and even to some extent controlled; but it cannot be changed. Until we receive our glorified bodies in the presence of the Lord, the struggle between the flesh and the Spirit will continue (Gal. 5:16-26).

It was the beginning of a new day for Abraham and Sarah, for Sarah was going to have a baby boy!

"Your father, Abraham, rejoiced to see My day," said Jesus; "and he saw it, and was glad" (John 8:56).

So As by Fire

Never in the field of human conflict was so much owed by so many to so few."

Sir Winston Churchill spoke those words to the British House of Commons on August 20, 1940. He reviewed the first year of the war and then paid special tribute to the brave Royal Air Force fighter pilots who were "turning the tide of the World War by their prowess and their devotion."

The citizens of Great Britain *knew* what the Royal Air Force was doing for them, but the citizens of Sodom and Gomorrah and the other cities of the plain did not know that three persons—Abraham, Lot, and Jesus Christ—stood between them and total destruction.

1. Abraham, the friend of God (Gen. 18)

Abraham is given this special title in 2 Chronicles 20:7; Isaiah 41:8; and James 2:23; and he is the only person in the Bible to have it. Jesus called Lazarus His friend (John 11:11), and He calls "friends" all who believe on Him and obey Him (15:13-15). As His friends, we can share His love and fellowship, and we can know His will. "If we are beset by an unseen foe," wrote Vance Havner, "we are also befriended by an Unseen Friend. Great is our adversary but greater is our Ally."

Friendship involves ministry; and in this chapter you will find Abraham ministering in three different areas: to the Lord (18:1-8), to his home (18:9-15), and to a lost world (18:16-33).

He ministered to the Lord (Gen. 18:1-8). All ministry must first be to the Lord; for if we fail to be a blessing to the Lord, we will never be a blessing to others. This was true of the Jewish priests (Ex. 28:1, 3-4, 41; 29:1) and of God's servants in the early church (Acts 13:1-2). "And whatever you do, do it heartily, as to the Lord and not to men ... for you serve the Lord Christ" (Col. 3:23-24, NKJV).

Abraham was taking his daily rest during the heat of the day when he saw three strangers approaching. Few people ever traveled when the sun was so hot, so Abraham was immediately both curious and courteous. Hospitality is the first law of the East, and Abraham faithfully obeyed it.

The three strangers were the Lord Jesus Christ and two of His angels (Gen. 18:1, 22; 19:1). There was nothing about their appearance that told Abraham who they were; but as he fellowshipped with them, he learned that he was entertaining royal visitors. His ministry to the Lord was so acceptable that we ought to follow his example today.

To begin with, he served the Lord *personally*. Remember, Abraham was ninety-nine years old and a wealthy sheikh, and he could have entrusted this task to his chief steward or one of his more than 300 servants (14:14). Instead, he decided to minister to his Lord personally.

He also ministered *immediately*. Abraham could have ignored them by pretending to be asleep, or he could have asked them to sit down and wait until he had finished his siesta. But Abraham was a man of faith, and faith does not delay when it comes to serving the Lord.

This chapter emphasizes that Abraham ministered to the

Lord *speedily*. He *ran* to meet the visitors (18:2) and *hastened* to tell Sarah to bake some bread (18:6). He *ran* to get a tender calf and saw to it that the young man *hastened* to dress the meat (18:7). Keep in mind that this is an old man running around in the heat of the day! Only after he had served his guests did Abraham stand still (18:8).

Abraham served the Lord *generously* and gave Him the best that he had. Sarah baked bread from "fine meal" (18:6), and the meat was "tender and good" (18:7). No leftovers or second-rate fare for such important guests! What a contrast to the priests in Malachi's day, who did not give God their best (Mal. 1:6-14).

Abraham's service was marked with *humility*. He bowed to his guests (Gen. 18:2), called himself a servant (18:3, 5), and called the feast only "a morsel of bread." He served the three visitors and then stood near to be available if needed. He interrupted a comfortable afternoon nap to become a servant to three strangers; but because of that service, he received tremendous blessings for himself and his wife.

Finally, he served the Lord *cooperatively* and involved the ministries of others. Sarah baked the bread; a young man dressed the meat; and no doubt other servants brought Abraham the butter and milk. "I would rather put ten men to work than do the work of ten men," said evangelist D.L. Moody; and he was right.

Over the years, I have studied the biographies of great Christians; and I have learned that dedicated servants of God encourage and inspire others to serve the Lord. D.L. Moody was used of God to enlist and assist a host of workers, including F.B. Meyer, G. Campbell Morgan, and R.A. Torrey. Paul Rader had a similar ministry in his generation, helping give birth to ministries still with us today. When we serve ourselves or our own ministries, our work perishes; but when we serve the Lord, He gives lasting and abundant fruit (John 12:20-28).

Before leaving this section, I should say a word about the importance of Christian hospitality. In this day of convenient motels and hotels, we rarely think about what it means to entertain strangers (Heb. 13:1-2); but hospitality is an important part of Christian ministry (Rom. 12:13; 1 Peter 4:9). In fact, "given to hospitality" is one of the requirements for leadership in the local church (1 Tim. 3:2; Titus 1:8). By lovingly serving others, we serve Jesus Christ our Lord (Matt. 25:34-40), and we promote the spread of God's truth (3 John 5-8).

He ministered to his wife (Gen 18:9-15). Because Abraham was faithful to the Lord, he became a channel of blessing to his wife and eventually to his family (Gen. 18:19). Sarah had an important role to play in the working out of God's plan of salvation for the world, and she did her part (Heb. 11:11; 1 Peter 3:1-7; Rom. 4:18-21). Sarah was now eighty-nine years old; yet she was still a desirable woman with charm and beauty (Gen. 20), partly because her husband loved her and treated her like the princess that she was.

The Lord had come all the way from heaven to give Abraham and Sarah an announcement: At that same time next year, Sarah would give birth to the promised son! The news was so incredible that Sarah laughed and questioned whether such a thing could happen to two elderly people. Abraham's laughter had been born out of joyful faith (17:17); but Sarah's laughter was marked by unbelief, even though she tried to deny it.

Of course, whenever we doubt God, we are questioning both His veracity and His ability. Does He keep His promises? Does He have the power to do what He says He will do? The answer to both questions is yes! (See Rom. 4:20-21.)

"Is anything too hard for the Lord?" (Gen. 18:14) Of course not! If you need proof, then listen to Job (42:2), Jeremiah (32:17 and 27), the Angel Gabriel (Luke 1:37), and the

Apostle Paul (Eph. 3:20-21). If God makes a promise, you can be sure He has the power to fulfill it; and He will remain faithful even if we are faithless (2 Tim. 2:13). Sarah eventually repented and, with her husband, trusted God; and He gave them the promised son.

The husband who ministers to the Lord will find himself ministering to the members of his own family, especially his wife. He will be a source of blessing in the home. When we study Genesis 19, we will see the contrast in Lot, a worldly man who had no spiritual influence in his own home.

He ministered to a lost world (Gen 18:16-33). Abraham belonged to that select company of God's people known as *intercessors,* individuals like Moses, Samuel, Elijah, Jeremiah, the apostles, and our Lord Himself. In fact, our Lord's ministry today in heaven is a ministry of intercession (Rom. 8:34); so we are never more like our Lord than when we are interceding for others. It is not enough for us to be a blessing to our Lord and our home; we must also seek to win a lost world and bring sinners to the Savior.

Charles Spurgeon said: "If they [lost sinners] will not hear you speak, they cannot prevent your praying. Do they jest at your exhortations? They cannot disturb you at your prayers. Are they far away so that you cannot reach them? Your prayers can reach them. Have they declared that they will never listen to you again, nor see your face? Never mind, God has a voice which they must hear. Speak to Him, and He will make them feel. Though they now treat you despitefully, rendering evil for your good, follow them with your prayers. Never let them perish for lack of your supplications" (*Metropolitan Pulpit,* vol. 18, pp. 263–264).

The Lord and the two angels left Abraham's camp and started toward Sodom, but the Lord lingered while the angels went on (Gen. 18:16, 22; 19:1). In the first half of the chapter, Abraham is running here and there; but in the last half, he is standing reverently before the Lord and interceding for Lot and the other people in Sodom. Blessed are the balanced!

An intercessor must know the Lord personally and be obedient to His will. He must be close enough to the Lord to learn His "secrets" and know what to pray about (Amos 3:7; Ps. 25:14). The Lord's words "I know him" (Gen. 18:19) mean "I have chosen him, and he is My intimate friend" (John 15:15). Abraham knew more about Sodom's future than the citizens themselves, including Lot. It is the separated believer who shares God's secrets.

Sarah and the servants helped Abraham when he prepared a meal for the three visitors; but when it came to the ministry of intercession, Abraham had to serve alone. Abraham drew near to the Lord (James 4:8), and the Hebrew word means "to come to court to argue a case." Abraham was burdened for Lot and Lot's family, as well as for the lost sinners in the five cities of the plain; and he had to share that burden with the Lord.

Abraham's prayer was based not on the mercy of God but on the justice of God. "Shall not the Judge of all the earth do right?" (Gen. 18:25; see Deut. 32:4) A just and holy God could not destroy righteous believers with wicked unbelievers; and Lot was a believer (2 Peter 2:6-9), even though his actions and words seemed to belie the fact.

The cities of Sodom and Gomorrah were exceedingly wicked (Gen. 13:13) because the men of these cities were given over to sexual practices that were contrary to nature (Gen. 19:5; Jude 7; Rom. 1:27). The words "sodomy" and "sodomize" are synonyms for these homosexual practices. The men did not try to hide their sin (Isa. 3:9). Nor would they repent (Jer. 23:14). The sudden destruction of Sodom and Gomorrah is used in Scripture as an example of God's righteous judgment on sinners (Isa. 1:9; 3:9; Lam. 4:6; Zeph. 2:9; 2 Peter 2:6ff), and Jesus used it as a warning for people in the end times (Luke 17:28-32).

But why would Abraham want God to spare such wicked people? Far better that they should be wiped off the face of the earth! Of course, Abraham's first concern was for Lot and his family. In fact, Abraham had already rescued the people of Sodom solely because of Lot (Gen. 14:12-16), though none of the citizens seemed to appreciate what he had done for them. They all went right back into the old way of life and did not heed the warning of God.

But even apart from Lot's situation (and he should not have been in Sodom in the first place), *Abraham did not want to see all those people die and be lost forever.* God is "not willing that any should perish" (2 Peter 3:9), and He "will have all men to be saved" (1 Tim. 2:4). "I have no pleasure in the death of the wicked, but that the wicked turn from his way and live" (Ezek. 33:11). The issue is not what kind of sins people commit, though some sins are certainly worse than others, but that "the wages of sin is death" (Rom. 6:23) and beyond that death is an eternal hell. Intercessors must have compassionate hearts and a deep concern for the salvation of the lost, no matter what their sins may be. (See 9:1-3; 10:1.)

We must not get the idea that Abraham argued with the Lord, because he did not. He was very humble before the Lord as he presented his case (Gen. 18:27, 30-32). Abraham was sure that there were at least ten believers in the city.

Never underestimate the importance of even a small number of believers. As few as ten people would have saved a whole city from destruction! If Lot had won only his own family to faith in the Lord, judgment would have been averted. Your personal witness today is important to God, no matter how insignificant you may feel.

2. Lot, the friend of the world (Gen. 19)
This chapter records the sad consequences of Lot's spiritual decline; then Lot passes off the scene while Abraham's story

continues (see 1 John 2:17). Abraham was the friend of God, but Lot was the friend of the world (see James 4:4); and the contrasts between these two men are easy to see.

Locations (Gen. 19:1). When the heavenly contingent came to visit Abraham, he was at his tent door; but Lot was sitting in the gate of a wicked city. Abraham was a pilgrim and stranger, only passing through this world; but Lot had gradually abandoned his tent and settled down in Sodom. Instead of keeping his eyes on the heavenly city (Heb. 11:10, 14-16), Lot looked toward Sodom and began to walk by sight (Gen. 13:10-11). Then he moved his tent near Sodom (13:12), and finally he moved into Sodom (14:12). Lot's location in the gate indicates that he was a man of some authority, for that was where official business was conducted (Ruth 4:1ff).

Had Lot gone to Sodom because God directed him, his being there would have fulfilled divine purposes. After all, God put Joseph in Egypt, Daniel in Babylon, and Esther in Persia; and their presence turned out to be a blessing. Worldliness is not a matter of physical geography but of heart attitude (1 John 2:15-17). *Lot's heart was in Sodom long before his body arrived there.* No doubt he got his first love for the world when he went to Egypt with Abraham (Gen. 13:1, 10), and he never overcame it.

Times (Gen. 19:1). It was early afternoon when the Lord and His angels visited Abraham (18:1), but it was evening when the angels entered Sodom. Abraham was "walking in the light" while Lot was "walking in darkness" (1 John 1:5-10).

Visitors (Gen. 19:1). Only the two angels visited Lot, for the Lord could not fellowship with Lot and his family as He did with Abraham and Sarah. Even though Lot was a believer, his life was such that the Lord did not feel "at home" with him. It is the separated believer who enjoys the close walk

(2 Cor. 6:14-18) and communion (John 14:21-24) with the Lord. Greek scholar Kenneth Wuest translated Paul's prayer in Ephesians 3:17 "that the Christ might finally settle down and feel completely at home in your hearts through your faith" (WUEST). Unlike Abraham, Lot had no tent or altar; and the Lord could not fellowship with him.

Hospitality (Gen. 19:2-11). Lot called himself a "servant," but you do not see him *hastening* to prepare a meal as Abraham did; nor did he stand by to see what further service he could render. But the arrival of the men of the city at the door for immoral purposes was the climax of the evening. ("Bring them out to us so that we can have sex with them" is the NIV translation of 19:5.) Lot was willing to sacrifice his two unmarried daughters to the lust of the crowd (see Jud. 19), but the angels intervened. What had happened to Lot's personal values that he would offer his daughters to satisfy the sensual appetites of a mob? (In contrast, Abraham would offer his son to the Lord.)

Messages (Gen. 19:12-13). God's message to Abraham was a joyful one: he and Sarah would have the promised son within a year. But the message to Lot was frightening: God was going to destroy Sodom and everything in it! God would have spared the city had the angels found ten believers; but since that was not possible, God mercifully rescued the believers they did find (19:16). God's message to the lost world is that judgment is coming, but His promise to His own people is that He will rescue them (1 Thes. 5:1-11; 2 Peter 2:4-10).

Influence (Gen. 19:14). Because of his faith and obedience, Abraham was a blessing to his home and to the whole world. Because of his worldliness, Lot had no spiritual influence either in the city or in his own home. His married daughters and their husbands laughed at him and refused to leave the city. Even his wife was so in love with Sodom that she had to take one last look, and that look killed her (Gen. 19:26; Luke 17:32). Lot's two unmarried daughters accompanied him out of the city; but they ended up in a cave, getting their father drunk and committing incest with him. After separating from Abraham, Lot had allowed his character to deteriorate; and his influence declined with it.

Attitudes (Gen. 19:15-26). The first time God rescued Lot, he was a prisoner of war (14:12, 16); and he went right back into Sodom. That painful experience should have warned him that he was out of the will of God; but if Lot heard the warning, he certainly did not heed it. Now God has to take Lot *by the hand* and forcibly drag him out of Sodom! First, Lot lingered; then he argued; then he begged to be allowed to go his own way. Instead of being grateful for God's mercy and obeying his rescuers, Lot resisted them and created trouble for them. In contrast, Abraham obeyed God's will even to the point of offering up his own son.

Consequences (Gen. 19:27-38). The result of the Lord's visit to Abraham was new hope and excitement as Abraham and Sarah joyfully anticipated the birth of a son. Lot, however, lost everything when Sodom was destroyed; and he himself was saved "yet as by fire" (1 Cor. 3:15). His daughters gave birth to two sons, whose descendants would be enemies to the Jewish nation. Abraham saw the cities of the plain destroyed (Ps. 91:8) and knew that God had not found ten righteous people. But God delivered Lot *because of Abraham* (Gen. 19:29). It was wholly a matter of God's grace and mercy (19:19).

Lot was conformed to the world (Rom. 12:2). All that he lived for went up in smoke and was buried under ruins somewhere in the area around the Dead Sea. Lot is a warning to all believers not to love the world, become friendly with the world, or be stained by the world (James 1:27), because the day of reckoning finally comes.

3. Jesus, the Friend of sinners

While it is true that the destruction of Sodom and Gomorrah is an example of God's righteous judgment (Jude 7), it is also true that God's love for lost sinners is clearly seen in this story. Jesus certainly did not approve of the lifestyle of the men of Sodom, but He came to save sinners just like those in Sodom and Gomorrah (Matt. 9:9-17). When He ministered on earth, He was known as "a Friend of tax collectors and sinners" (11:19)—*and He was!*

Consider our Lord's love for the people of the wicked cities of the plain. To begin with, He was long-suffering toward them as He beheld their sin (Gen. 18:20; 19:13). Just as Abel's blood cried out to God from the ground (4:10), so the sins of the people cried out from the wicked cities. God is long-suffering and holds back His judgment so that sinners will have time to repent (2 Peter 3:1-9).

Not only was our Lord long-suffering, but He was willing to listen to Abraham's intercession and consider sparing Sodom for ten righteous people. When the time came for the cities to be burned up, He sent His angels to rescue Lot and his family *even though the ten righteous people could not be found!* "But where sin abounded, grace abounded much more" (Rom. 5:20, NKJV). Did Lot deserve to be delivered? Of course not! *But do any of us deserve to be saved from the wrath to come? Of course not!*

The most amazing thing is that Jesus Christ *died for the sinners in Sodom and Gomorrah!* "For Christ also has suffered once for sins, the just for the unjust, that He might bring us to God" (1 Peter 3:18, NKJV). Christ did not die for good people, because there are none. He died for the *ungodly* (Rom. 5:6) and for *sinners* (5:8). We may not have committed the same sins as the people of Sodom and Gomorrah, but we are sinners just the same; and apart from faith in Jesus Christ, we cannot be saved from the judgment to come.

83

The situation is no different today. Jesus is still the Friend of sinners and will save all who come to Him in true repentance and faith. He needs intercessors and witnesses who will pray and tell lost sinners that Jesus died for them and they can make a new beginning if they will trust Him.

The inhabitants of the cities of the plain had no idea that they were awakening that morning to the last day of their lives (Gen. 19:23). Life was going on as usual, and then the fire fell (Luke 17:26-30).

When the judgment comes, will you be like Abraham and not have to worry about the wrath of God? Or, like Lot, will you be saved "as by fire"? Or, like the people of Sodom, will you be lost forever?

"Seek ye the Lord while He may be found, call ye upon Him while He is near; Let the wicked forsake his way, and the unrighteous man his thoughts, and let him return unto the Lord, and He will have mercy upon him; and to our God; for He will abundantly pardon" (Isa. 55:6-7).

Abraham the Neighbor

*W*e make our friends and our enemies," wrote G.K. Chesterton, "but God appoints our next-door neighbor." Someone has defined a neighbor as "a person who can get into your house in a minute, but it takes two hours to get him out." Neighbors can be a great source of blessing and even grow closer to us than some of our relatives. "Better is a neighbor that is near than a brother far off," counseled Solomon (Prov. 27:10). However, neighbors can be a problem at times, whether believers or unbelievers. In fact, *we* can be a problem to our neighbors!

We usually think of Abraham as a man who was always performing great exploits of faith, and we forget that his daily life was somewhat routine. He had to take care of a pregnant wife and a young son, and he needed to manage great flocks and herds and handle the business affairs of the camp. Abraham and his chief steward were responsible for settling the daily disputes and making important decisions.

In addition, there were neighbors to deal with—like Abimelech, the king of Gerar. In Abraham's dealings with his neighbors, the patriarch is seen first as a troublemaker (Gen. 20) and then as a peacemaker (21:22-34). As we study these two experiences, we can learn how to relate positively to those who are outside the faith and be better witnesses to them (Col. 4:5; 1 Thes. 4:12; 1 Tim. 3:7).

1. Abraham the troublemaker (Gen. 20).

If you did not know who Abraham was, and you read this chapter for the first time, which of the two men would you say was the believer? Surely not Abraham, the liar! It was not Abraham who showed integrity, and it was not Abraham whom God kept from sinning. What Abraham did was selfish, but Abimelech responded with generosity. If anybody reveals excellent character, it is Abimelech and not Abraham, "the friend of God."

But before you draw some unwarranted conclusions, take time to consider the facts revealed in this event. Abraham's failures were tragic, but from them we learn some valuable lessons to help us in our walk of faith.

Believers do sin. This chapter would be an embarrassment to us except for one thing: The Bible tells the truth about *all* people, and that includes God's people. It does not hide the fact that Noah got drunk and exposed himself (Gen. 9:20-23), or that Moses lost his temper (Num. 20:1-13), or that David committed adultery and plotted the death of a valiant soldier (2 Sam. 11). Peter denied the Lord three times (Matt. 26:69-75), and Barnabas lapsed into false doctrine (Gal. 2:13).

These things are recorded, not to encourage us to sin, but to warn us to beware of sin. After all, if these great men of faith disobeyed the Lord, then we "ordinary saints" had better be very careful! "Therefore let him who thinks he stands take heed lest he fall" (1 Cor. 10:12, NKJV).

Why did Abraham sin?

For one thing, though Abraham had a sinful nature, he had been justified by faith (Gen. 15:6). God gave him a new name (from "Abram" to "Abraham"), but that did not change his

old nature. "If we say that we have no sin, we deceive ourselves, and the truth is not in us" (1 John 1:8). Because of
the indwelling of the Holy Spirit (Gal. 5:16ff) and the work of
Christ on the cross (Rom. 6), believers can have victory over
the old nature; but this is not automatic. We must walk in the
Spirit if we hope to overcome temptation.

That leads to a second consideration: Abraham moved into
"enemy territory." After living at Hebron ("fellowship") for
perhaps twenty years, he then decided to go to the land of
the Philistines. Gerar is just within Philistine country, but it
was still a dangerous place to be. Perhaps it was the destruction of Sodom and Gomorrah that caused Abraham to want to
move; but whatever his motive was, the decision was not a
wise one. True, Abraham did not go down to Egypt as he had
done before (Gen. 12). He was still within the boundaries of
the land God promised to give him, but his move put him in a
dangerous position. "Watch and pray, lest you enter into
temptation" (Matt. 26:41, NKJV).

After arriving in Gerar, Abraham began to walk by sight
and not by faith; for he began to be afraid (Gen. 20:11). Fear
of man and faith in God cannot dwell together in the same
heart. "The fear of man brings a snare, but whoever trusts in
the Lord shall be safe" (Prov. 29:25, NKJV). Abraham forgot
that his God was "the Almighty God" (Gen. 17:1) who could
do anything (18:14) and who had covenanted to bless Abraham and Sarah.

But the basic cause of Abraham's failure was the sad fact
that he and Sarah *had failed to judge this sin when they had
dealt with it in Egypt.* (See 12:10-20.) They had admitted their
sin to Pharaoh and confessed it to God, but the fact that it
surfaced again indicates that they did not judge the sin and
forsake it (Prov. 28:13). In fact, the sin had grown worse; for
now *Sarah shared in telling the lie* (Gen. 20:5). A home kept
together by a lie is in bad shape indeed.

A lighthearted admission of sin is not the same as a brokenhearted confession of sin (Ps. 51:17). If our attitude is right, we will hate our sins, loathe ourselves for having sinned (Ezek. 6:9; 36:31), and despise the very memory of our sins. People who remember their sins with pleasure and "enjoy them again" in their minds have never judged their sins or seen how sinful their sins really are. The father of American psychology, William James, wrote, "For him who confesses, shams are over and realities have begun."

Abraham and Sarah had convinced themselves that they were not telling a lie at all. It was only a "half-truth" (Gen. 20:12), and half-truths are not supposed to be as wicked as outright lies. *They are worse!* "A lie consists in the motive quite as much as in the actual words," wrote F.B. Meyer. A half-truth has just enough fact in it to make it plausible and just enough deception to make it dangerous.

So, believers do sin; but that does not disannul their faith or destroy their salvation, though it may discredit their testimony. Abraham was still a child of God even though his witness for the Lord had been greatly weakened. However, Abimelech was in a more dangerous position than Abraham; *for Abimelech was under a sentence of death* (20:3, 7).

Abimelech was a man of integrity; and when God spoke to him, he obeyed. He had many fine qualities; but he was not a believer, and therefore he was a dead man (Eph. 2:1-3). This is not to minimize the enormity of Abraham's sin, for a believer should not do what Abraham did. But Abraham and Abimelech had two different standings before God: One was saved, and the other was lost.

So, any unsaved person who wants to use Genesis 20 as "ammunition" against believers ("You're all hypocrites!") had better consider his or her spiritual condition before God. If unsaved people accept what the Bible says about Abraham, that he lied, then they must also accept what the Bible says about them: They are dead in trespasses and sins. In spite of his disobedience, Abraham was accepted before God; but Abimelech was rejected and under divine condemnation (John 3:18-21). God chastened Abraham, but He condemned Abimelech.

When believers sin, they suffer. Charles Spurgeon said, "God does not allow His children to sin successfully." When we deliberately disobey God, we suffer both from the consequences of our sins and from the chastening hand of God, unless we repent and submit (Heb. 12:5-11). God in His grace will forgive our sins (1 John 1:5-10), but God in His sovereignty must allow sin to produce a sad harvest (Gal. 6:7). Read Psalms 32 and 51 to see what happened to David physically and spiritually because he would not repent and confess his sins to the Lord.

It took only a few seconds for Abraham to tell a lie, but that lie was more than sounds and puffs of breath in the air. That lie became a seed that was planted and grew and brought forth bitter fruit. God hates lies (Prov. 6:17; 12:22). He is a God of truth (Deut. 32:4), the Spirit is the Spirit of Truth (John 14:17), and the Word is the Word of Truth (James 1:18). "A lying tongue is but for a moment," wrote Matthew Henry. "Truth is the daughter of time; and in time, it will out."

What did this one lie cost Abraham? To begin with, it cost him *character.* Phillips Brooks said, "The purpose of life is the building of character through truth." God is not just "saving souls" and taking people to heaven. Through the trials and testing of life, He is making saved people more like Jesus Christ and thereby glorifying Himself. Abraham stopped asking "What is right?" and began asking "What is safe?" and this led to his downfall. Once the salt has lost its taste, how do you restore it?

He also lost his *testimony.* How could Abraham talk to his pagan neighbors about the God of truth when he himself had told a lie? Lot lost his witness in Sodom, and Abraham lost his witness in Gerar. "A bad man's example has little influence over good men," wrote James Strahan in *Hebrew Ideals* (Kregel, 1982, p. 141). "But the bad example of a good man, eminent in station and established in reputation, has an enormous power for evil."

Imagine how humiliated Abraham was when Abimelech called him in, confronted him, and rebuked him. It is hard enough to submit to the rebuke of a Christian brother or sister, but to accept rebuke from an unsaved person demands a great deal of honesty and humility. "You have done things to me that should not be done" (Gen. 20:9, NIV). Those words cut deep! Christians must be careful how they relate to those who are "outside" (Col. 4:5; 1 Thes. 4:12).

He lost his *ministry;* for instead of being a source of blessing (Gen. 12:1-3), he was the cause of judgment. No babies were born during Abraham's sojourn in Gerar (12:17-18). When a child of God gets out of the will of God, the discipline of God usually follows. Jonah caused a storm that nearly wrecked the ship (Jonah 1); Achan brought defeat to the army (Josh. 7); and David brought sorrow to his family (2 Sam. 12:10).

Abraham almost lost *Sarah and Isaac.* In that day, a king had the right to take into his harem any single woman who pleased him. Abimelech thought Sarah was a single woman, so he took her; and were it not for the intervention of God, the king would have had normal relations with her. What the king did threatened God's great plan of salvation, so the Lord had to act to protect Sarah and Isaac. Whenever we do something that forces God to intervene miraculously, we are tempting God; and tempting God is sin (Deut. 6:16; Matt. 4:7).

Perhaps one of the saddest consequences of Abraham's sin was *Isaac's repetition of it years later* (Gen. 26:7-11). It is sad when our sins affect outsiders, but it is sadder still when our sins are duplicated in our own families. In fact, Isaac's lie was worse than his father's because Sarah really was Abraham's half sister, while Rebekah was only Isaac's cousin.

When believers sin, they are disciplined by God until they come to a place of repentance and confession. This discipline is not enjoyable, but it is profitable; and in the end, it produces happiness and holiness to the glory of God.

Sinning believers can be forgiven and restored. While God did not defend Abraham's sin, He did defend Abraham and so control circumstances that His servant was not completely defeated. In fact, God called Abraham a prophet and made it clear that Abraham's intercession was the only thing that stood between Abimelech and death (Gen. 20:7). The fact that God answered Abraham's prayer for Abimelech is evidence that Abraham had confessed his sins and the Lord had forgiven him (Ps. 66:18-20).

God does not reject His children when they sin any more than a parent rejects a disobedient son or daughter (Isa. 49:13-16). Abraham was justified by faith and had a righteous standing before God (Rom. 4:1-5). Justification does not change; we are accepted in Jesus Christ no matter what we are in ourselves (2 Cor. 5:17, 21; Eph. 1:6). Of course, the fact that we are justified before God means there will be a change in our lives; for "faith without works is dead" (James 2:20). But our *position in Christ* (justification) is not altered by our *practice on earth* (sanctification).

The important thing is that we deal with our sins humbly and honestly, confess them to God, judge them and forsake them, and claim His promises of forgiveness (1 John 1:9; Micah 7:18-19; Isa. 55:6-13). Abraham and Sarah made a new beginning, and so can you.

2. Abraham the peacemaker (Gen. 21:22-34)

Swearing (Gen. 21:22-24). As many as four years may have passed since the events of Genesis 20; and during that time, it was evident that God was blessing Abraham and Sarah. Whenever a believer is restored to fellowship with the Lord, God can bless once again. The purpose of discipline is restoration, and the purpose of restoration is ministry and blessing. Not only was Abraham's wealth increasing, but Isaac had been born; and this "miracle son" must have been the leading topic of conversation among the neighbors.

Abimelech was an official title rather than a personal name, so we cannot be sure that the Abimelech of this episode is the same man who previously rebuked Abraham. The fact that he wanted assurance of Abraham's fidelity indicates that the patriarch's deception had led to a lack of trust on the part of his neighbors. They wanted assurance that Abraham would "play fair" with them because he was such a powerful man.

What a testimony: "God is with you in all that you do" (21:22, NKJV). Abraham did not permit one lapse of faith to cripple him; he got right with God and made a new beginning. James Strahan said, "Men are not to be judged by the presence or absence of faults, but by the *direction* of their lives" (*Hebrew Ideals,* p. 142). God is willing to bless when we are in the place of blessing (Ps. 1:1-3).

While living at Hebron, Abraham had allied himself with some of the local leaders (Gen. 14:13); so there was no problem with entering into an agreement with Abimelech. It did not compromise Abraham's testimony. God's people cooperate with different people at different times for different purposes, and the discerning believer knows when any alliance is not in the will of God.

Reproving (Gen. 21:25-26). Water is still a very precious commodity in the Holy Land. Today, various methods of irrigation are used; but in Abraham's day, it was necessary to dig wells and guard them carefully. If you did not guard your well, your enemies might seize it or fill it up (26:18). Some of Abimelech's servants had seized Abraham's well, so the treaty between the two men had not done much good.

Abraham did the right thing and confronted his neighbor with the facts, but Abimelech declared that he knew nothing about it. Was he telling the truth? Only God knows, but Abraham made sure the problem would never appear again.

Witnessing (Gen. 21:27-32). The Hebrew word "to swear" means "to bind by seven things," and the words "swear" *(saba)* and "seven" *(seba)* are very similar. This time the two men went beyond merely giving their oath: They made a covenant that involved slaying animals (21:27; 15:9-10). As Abraham and Abimelech walked between the carcasses of the sacrifices, they were saying, in effect, "May God do to us and more if we fail to keep our covenant with each other." This was a serious matter.

But Abraham went a step further: He set aside seven very valuable ewe lambs as living witnesses that he had dug the well and the water belonged to him. He gave the lambs to Abimelech who would then guard them carefully. They were like "receipts" guaranteeing that Abraham owned the well. The name of the well (Beersheba means "well of the oath") was another witness to the transaction. Both men swore to uphold the covenant, and the problem was settled.

This entire transaction involved three elements: sacrifices (21:27), witnesses (21:28-30), and promises (21:31-32). You find these same elements in God's covenant with us through our Lord Jesus Christ, as outlined in Hebrews 10:1-18. First, there is the sacrifice of Jesus Christ on the cross (10:1-14); then, the witness of the Spirit within the believer (10:15); and finally, the promise of God's Word (10:16-18). Abraham's covenant with Abimelech only guaranteed possession of a well that provides water to sustain life. God's covenant with His people guarantees that we have the living water that gives everlasting life to all who will trust the Savior!

Planting (Gen. 21:33). This grove (or tamarisk tree) was

also a part of the covenant, a witness to the promises Abraham and Abimelech had made. The tamarisk is a shrub-like tree that has very hard wood and evergreen leaves. As he built an oasis, Abraham was certainly interested in ecology (water and trees); but even more, he was giving witness of what God had done for him. He had gone through a difficult experience in life and had left some blessings behind for others. He was like the pilgrims described in Psalm 84:6, who pass through the Valley of Baca ("weeping") and make it a place of springs that will refresh others.

Worshiping (Gen. 21:33). You could follow Abraham's journey by looking for the wells he dug and the altars he built (Gen. 12:7-8; 13:4, 18). He was not ashamed to build his altar in the presence of his neighbors and offer his worship to the Lord. A new name for God is introduced here: *El Olam,* "the Everlasting God." Abraham already knew *El Elyon* ("God Most High"—14:19, 22) and *El Shaddai* ("God Almighty, the All-Sufficient One"—17:1); but now he had a new name to use in his worship. It is important as we go through life that we learn more and more about God so we can worship Him better.

What an encouragement to know "the Everlasting God"! Wells would disappear, trees would be cut down, ewe lambs would grow up and die, altars would crumble, and treaties would perish; but the Everlasting God would remain. This Everlasting God had made an everlasting covenant with Abraham and his descendants (17:7, 13, 19), and He had given them the land of Canaan as an everlasting possession (17:8; 48:4). As Abraham faced the coming years, he knew that God would not change and that "underneath [were] the everlasting arms" (Deut. 33:27).

Waiting (Gen. 21:34). The "many days" of this verse could mean as much as ten to fifteen years, because Isaac was a young man when he accompanied Abraham to Mount Moriah

(Gen. 22). It must have been a peaceful time for Abraham, Sarah, and Isaac, and a time of great happiness as they watched their precious son grow up. Little did they know the great test that lay before them, but God was preparing them, and they would be ready.

GENESIS 21:1-21;
GALATIANS 4:21-31

"A Time to Weep, a Time to Laugh"

The Christian life is a land of hills and valleys," said Scottish preacher George Morrison, basing his words on Deuteronomy 11:11. Solomon expressed the same idea when he wrote in Ecclesiastes 3:4 that "[there is] a time to weep, and a time to laugh." Heaven is a place of unending joy; hell is a place of unending suffering; but while we are here on earth, we must expect both joy and sorrow, laughter and tears. You cannot have hills without valleys.

This is especially true of family life, for the same people who bring us joy can also bring us sorrow. Relationships can become strained and then change overnight, and we wonder what happened to a happy home. A Chinese proverb says, "Nobody's family can hang out the sign 'Nothing the matter here.' "

The coming of Isaac into their home brought both sorrow and joy to Abraham and Sarah. As you look at the persons involved in this important event, you can learn some valuable lessons about basic Christian doctrine and how to live the Christian life.

1. Abraham and Sarah: faith and promise (Gen. 21:1-7)
Sarah had borne the burden of childlessness for many years, a heavy burden indeed in that culture and at that time. People

must have smiled when they heard that her husband's name was Abraham, "father of a multitude." He was the father of *one* son, Ishmael, but that was far from a multitude; and Sarah had *never* given birth. But now all of her reproach was ended, and they were rejoicing in the arrival of their son.

But the birth of Isaac involved much more than parental joy, for his birth meant the *fulfillment of God's promise.* When God had called Abraham, He promised to make of him a great nation that would bless the whole world (12:1-3). Then He repeatedly promised to give the land of Canaan to Abraham's descendants (17:7) and to multiply them greatly (13:15-17). Abraham would be the father of the promised seed (15:4), and Sarah (not Hagar) would be the mother (17:19; 18:9-15). The birth of Isaac reminds us that God keeps His promises, in His own way, and in His own time. In spite of their occasional failures, Abraham and Sarah believed God; and God honored their faith (Heb. 11:8-11).

Isaac's birth also meant *the rewarding of patience.* Abraham and Sarah had to wait twenty-five years for their son to be born, because it is "through faith and patience [we] inherit the promises" (Heb. 6:12; see 10:36). Trusting God's promises not only gives you a blessing *at the end,* but it gives you a blessing *while you are waiting.* Just as Olympic athletes develop their skills as they practice hard long before the big event, so God's children grow in godliness and faith as they wait for the fulfillment of God's promises. Faith is a journey, and each happy destination is the beginning of a new journey. When God wants to build our patience, He gives us promises, sends us trials, and tells us to trust Him (James 1:1-8).

The birth of Isaac was certainly *the revelation of God's power.* That was one reason why God waited so long: He wanted Abraham and Sarah to be "as good as dead" so that their son's birth would be a miracle of God and not a marvel of human nature (Rom. 4:17-21). Abraham and Sarah experienced God's resurrection power in their lives because they yielded to Him and believed His Word. Faith in God's promises releases God's power (Eph. 3:20-21; Phil. 3:10), "for no word from God shall be void of power" (Luke 1:37, ASV).

Finally, the birth of Isaac was a step forward in the *accomplishing of God's purpose*. The future redemption of a lost world rested with a little baby boy! Isaac would beget Jacob, and Jacob would give the world the twelve tribes of Israel; and from Israel the promised Messiah would be born. Down through the centuries, some of the "living links" in the chain of promise may have seemed insignificant and weak; but they helped to fulfill the purposes of God.

You may wonder if what you do is really important to God and His work in this world; but it is, if you are faithful to trust His Word and do His will. The next time you feel defeated and discouraged, remember Abraham and Sarah; and remind yourself that *faith* and *promise* go together. God keeps His promises and gives you the power you need to do what He wants you to do. No matter how long you may have to wait, you can trust God to accomplish His purposes.

2. Isaac and Ishmael: Spirit and flesh (Gen. 21:8-11)
In Galatians 4:28-29, Paul makes it clear that Ishmael represents the believer's first birth (the flesh) and Isaac represents the second birth (the Spirit). Ishmael was "born of the flesh" because Abraham had not yet "died" and was still able to beget a son (Gen. 16). Isaac was "born of the Spirit" because by that time his parents were both "dead" and only God's power could have brought conception and birth. Ishmael was born first, because the natural comes before the spiritual (1 Cor. 15:46).

When you trust Jesus Christ, you experience a miracle birth from God (John 1:11-13), and it is the work of the Holy Spirit of God (John 3:1-8). Abraham represents *faith*, and Sarah represents *grace* (Gal. 4:24-26), so Isaac was born "by grace . . . through faith" (Eph. 2:8-9). This is the only way a lost sinner can enter the family of God (John 3:16-18).

It is worth noting that, in the biblical record, God often rejected the firstborn and accepted the second-born. He rejected Cain and chose Abel (Gen. 4:1-15). He rejected Ishmael, Abraham's firstborn, and chose Isaac. He bypassed Esau, Isaac's firstborn, and chose Jacob (Rom. 9:8-13); and He chose Ephraim instead of Manasseh (Gen. 48). In Egypt, the Lord condemned *all* the firstborn (Ex. 11–12) and spared only those who were "twice-born" because they were protected by faith in the blood of the lamb.

Isaac pictures the child of God not only in his birth but also in *the joy that he brought.* Isaac means "laughter," and this time it was not the laughter of unbelief (Gen. 18:9-15). In the parables recorded in Luke 15, Jesus emphasized the joy that results when lost sinners repent and come to the Lord. The shepherd rejoiced when he found the lost sheep, and the woman rejoiced when she found the lost coin; and they both asked their friends to rejoice with them. The father rejoiced when his prodigal son came home, and he invited the neighbors to a feast so they could share in his joy. There is even joy in heaven when sinners turn to God (Luke 15:7, 10).

Nowhere do we read that Ishmael caused great joy in Abraham's home. Abraham loved his son and wanted the best for him (Gen. 17:18). From before his birth, Ishmael was a source of painful trouble (Gen. 16); and after he matured, he caused even greater conflict in the family (21:9). The old nature is not able to produce the fruit of the Spirit, no matter how hard it tries (Gal. 5:16-26).

Note a third comparison between Isaac and the child of God: *He grew and was weaned* (Gen. 21:8). The new birth is not the end, but the beginning; and the believer must feed on God's Word and grow spiritually (Matt. 4:4; 1 Cor. 3:1-3; Heb.

5:12-14; 1 Peter 2:1-3; 2 Peter 3:18). As we mature in the Lord, we must "put away childish things" (1 Cor. 13:9-11) and allow God to "wean us" (Ps. 131) from temporary helps that can become permanent hindrances.

The mother weans the child because she loves the child and wants it to be free to grow up and not be dependent on her. But the child interprets her actions as an expression of rejection and hatred. The child clings to the comforts of the past as the mother tries to encourage the child to grow up and enter into the challenges of the future. The time comes in every Christian life when toys must be replaced by tools and selfish security by unselfish service (John 12:23-26).

Like every child of God, *Isaac experienced persecution* (Gen. 21:9; Gal. 4:29). Ishmael was apparently an obedient son *until Isaac entered the family,* and then the "flesh" began to oppose "the Spirit." It has well been said that the old nature knows no law but the new nature needs no law, and this is certainly illustrated in Abraham's two sons.

Jewish children were usually weaned at about age three, so Ishmael was probably seventeen years old at the time (Gen. 16:16). What arrogance that a boy of seventeen should torment a little boy of only three! But God had said that Ishmael would become "a wild donkey of a man" (16:12, NIV), and the prediction came true. The flesh and the Spirit are in conflict with each other and always will be until we see the Lord (Gal. 5:16-26).

When, like Isaac, you are born of the Spirit, *you are born rich* (Gen. 21:10). Isaac was the heir of all that his father owned, and God's children are "heirs of God, and joint heirs with Christ" (Rom. 8:17). Abraham cared for Ishmael while the boy was in the home, but "Abraham gave all that he had unto Isaac" (Gen. 25:5).

Finally, *Isaac was born free* while Ishmael was the son of a slave (Gal. 4:22). Freedom is one of the key themes in Galatians (5:1) and one of the key blessings in the Christian life (4:31). Of course, Christian freedom does not mean anarchy; for that is the worst kind of bondage. It means the freedom to be and to do all that God has for us in Jesus Christ. "No man in this world attains to freedom from any slavery except by entrance into some higher servitude," said Phillips Brooks; and that "higher servitude" is personal surrender to Jesus Christ. No one is more free than the child of God who delights in God's will and does it from the heart.

3. Sarah and Hagar: grace and Law (Gen. 21:9-13)

Sarah was wrong when she told Abraham to marry Hagar (Gen. 16:1-2), but she was right when she told Abraham to send Hagar and Ishmael out of the camp. The Apostle Paul saw in this event an allegory involving the Law of Moses and the grace of God (Gal. 4:21-31). Sarah represents grace (the heavenly Jerusalem), and Hagar represents Law (the earthly Jerusalem under bondage). The lesson is simply that God's children are to live under the blessings of grace and not the bondage of Law.

The conflicts in Abraham's home could have been solved four ways. Isaac could have been sent away, but that would mean rejecting the promises of God and all that God had planned for the future. Isaac and Ishmael could have lived together, but that would mean constant conflict. Ishmael's nature could have been changed to make him more agreeable, but that would have required a miracle. "That which is born of the flesh is flesh" (John 3:6), *and it always will be flesh.* The only solution was to send Ishmael and his mother out of the camp and make Isaac the sole heir.

When you consider the facts about Hagar, you will better understand the relationship between Law and grace in the Christian life.

To begin with, *Hagar was Abraham's second wife.* She was

added alongside Sarah. Likewise, the Law was "added" alongside God's already existing promises and was temporary (Gal. 3:19, 24-25). God did not start with Law; He started with grace. His relationship to Adam and Eve was based on grace, not Law, even though He did test them by means of one simple restriction (Gen. 2:15-17). The redemption of Israel from Egypt was an act of God's grace, as was His provision, the sacrifices, and priesthood. Before Moses gave the Law, Israel was already in a covenant relationship with God ("married to God") through His promises to the patriarchs (Ex. 19:1-8).

Second, *Hagar was a servant.* "Wherefore, then, serveth the Law?" Paul asks in Galatians 3:19, and he gives the answer. The Law was God's servant (a "schoolmaster" or "child tutor") to keep the infant nation of Israel under control and prepare them for the coming of the Redeemer (3:24-25; 4:1-5). The Law was given to reveal sin (Rom. 3:20) but not to redeem us from sin. Grace does not serve Law; it is Law that serves grace! The Law reveals our need for grace, and grace saves us completely apart from the works of the Law (Rom. 3:20, 28).

A third fact is obvious: *Hagar was never supposed to bear a child.* The Law cannot give what only Jesus Christ can give: life (Gal. 3:21), righteousness (2:21), the Holy Spirit (3:2), or an eternal inheritance (3:18). All of these blessings come only "by grace [Sarah] . . . through faith [Abraham]" (Eph. 2:8-9).

This leads to a fourth fact: *Hagar gave birth to a slave.* If you decide to live under the Law, then you become a child of Hagar, a slave; for the Law produces bondage and not freedom. The first doctrinal battle the church had to fight was on this very issue; and it was decided that sinners are saved wholly by grace, apart from keeping the Law of Moses (Acts 15:1-32). Legalists in the church today are turning sons into slaves and replacing freedom with slavery (Gal. 4:1-11); yet,

God calls us to freedom! (5:1)

Hagar was cast out. There was no compromise: She was cast out completely and permanently and took Ishmael with her. Instead of subduing the flesh, the Law arouses the flesh (Rom. 7:7-12) because "the strength of sin is the Law" (1 Cor. 15:56). Believers don't need to put themselves under some kind of religious law in order to become Christlike, for they are already complete and full in Christ (Col. 2:8-23) and have the Holy Spirit to enable them to overcome sin (Rom. 8:1-4).

Finally, *Hagar never married again.* God gave His Law to the Jewish nation *only* and never gave it to the Gentiles or to the church. Nine of the Ten Commandments are quoted in the Epistles as applying to believers today, and we should obey them; but we are not commanded to obey the ceremonial laws that were given only to Israel (see Rom. 13:8-10). Paul affirms that it is love that fulfills the Law. When we love God and love one another, we *want* to obey God; and in the Spirit's power, we do what is right.

Before leaving this section, we should notice that there is a "lawful use of the Law" (1 Tim. 1:1-11). While the Law cannot save us or sanctify us, it does reveal the holiness of God and the awfulness of sin. The ceremonial part of the Law illustrates the person and work of Jesus Christ. The Law is a mirror that helps us see our sins (James 1:21-25), but you do not wash your face in the mirror! It is also a mirror that reveals the glory of Jesus Christ; and as we meditate on Him, we can be transformed to become more like Him (2 Cor. 3:18). Any religious system that leads you into bondage is not magnifying the New Testament Gospel of the grace of God (2 Cor. 3:17; John 8:31-36).

4. God and Hagar: promise and provision (Gen. 21:12-21)
It was "grievous" (21:11-12) for Abraham to say good-bye to his son, but this was God's command, and he had to obey. Little did he realize that his obedience was preparation for an

even greater test when he would have to put Isaac on the altar. The word translated "grievous" means "to shake violently," like curtains blowing in the wind. Abraham was deeply moved within and perhaps somewhat displeased at this turn of events.

However, God did not abandon Hagar and Ishmael; for Ishmael was the son of Abraham, God's friend (21:13). If Ishmael and Hagar had any bad feelings toward Abraham, they were certainly in the wrong; everything God did for them was because of His faithfulness to Abraham. The Lord reaffirmed His promise that Ishmael would become a great nation (21:13, 18; 17:20), and He kept His promise (25:12-16). The Arab world is a force to be reckoned with today, and it all began with Ishmael.

In spite of the pictures in some Sunday School papers and Bible story books, Ishmael was a teenager and not a child when this event took place. The word translated "child" can refer to a fetus (Ex. 21:22), newborn children (1:17-18), young children (1 Kings 17:21-23), or even young adults (12:8-14; Dan. 1:4ff). In this case, it refers to a boy at least fifteen years old.

Ishmael and Hagar got lost in the wilderness, their water ran out, and they gave up in despair. This experience was quite different from the time Hagar first met God in the wilderness (Gen. 16:7ff). Sixteen years before, she had found a fountain of water; but now she saw no hope at all. Apparently Hagar had forgotten the promises God had made concerning her son; but Ishmael must have remembered them, for he called on the Lord for help. God heard the lad's cries and rescued them both for Abraham's sake.

So often in the trials of life we fail to see the divine provisions God has made for us, and we forget the promises He has made to us. We open our hands to receive what we think we need instead of asking Him to open our eyes to see what we already have. The answer to most problems is close at hand, if only we have eyes to see (John 6:1-13; 21:1-6).

Hagar is certainly a picture of the needy multitudes in the world today: wandering, weary, thirsty, blind, and giving up in despair. How we need to tell them the good news that the water of life is available and the well is not far away! (John 4:10-14; 7:37-39) God is kind and gracious to all who call on Him, because of His beloved Son, Jesus Christ.

Horatius Bonar wrote these words:

> I heard the voice of Jesus say,
> "Behold, I freely give
> The living water; thirsty one,
> Stoop down, and drink, and live."
> I came to Jesus, and I drank
> Of that life-giving stream;
> My thirst was quenched, my soul revived,
> And now I live in Him.

"If any man thirst, let him come unto Me, and drink" (John 7:37). "And whosoever will, let him take the water of life freely" (Rev. 22:17).

The Greatest Test of All

An inscription on a cathedral clock reads:

> When, as a child, I laughed and wept,
>   Time crept.
> When, as a youth, I dreamed and talked,
>   Time walked.
> When I became a full-grown man,
>   Time ran.
> And later, as I older grew,
>   Time flew.
> Soon I shall find, while traveling on,
>   Time gone.

At the age of 75, Abraham enrolled in the "School of Faith." Now he was over 100, and he was still having soul-stretching experiences. We are never too old to face new challenges, fight new battles, and learn new truths. When we stop learning, we stop growing; and when we stop growing, we stop living.

"The first forty years of life give us the text," wrote Arthur Schopenhauer, "and the next thirty supply the commentary." For the Christian believer, the text is Habakkuk 2:4: "The just shall live by his faith." The "commentary" is being written as we listen to God and obey His directions a day at a time. Sad to say, some people understand neither the text nor the commentary, and their lives are ended before they have really started to live.

Genesis 22 records the greatest test that Abraham ever faced. True, it also presents a beautiful picture of our Lord's sacrifice at Calvary; but the main lesson is *obedient faith that overcomes in the trials of life.* Abraham teaches us how to face and handle the tests of life to the glory of God. Consider five simple instructions.

1. Expect tests from God (Gen. 22:1-2)

In the "School of Faith" we must have occasional tests, or we will never know where we are spiritually. Abraham had his share of tests right from the beginning. First was the "family test," when he had to leave his loved ones and step out by faith to go to a new land (11:27–12:5). This was followed by the "famine test," which Abraham failed because he doubted God and went down to Egypt for help (12:10–13:4).

Once back in the land, Abraham passed the "fellowship test" when he gave Lot first choice in using the pastureland (13:5-18). He also passed the "fight test" when he defeated the kings (14:1-16) and the "fortune test" when he said no to Sodom's wealth (14:17-24). But he failed the "fatherhood test" when Sarah got impatient with God and suggested that Abraham have a child by Hagar (Gen. 16). When the time came to send Ishmael away, Abraham passed the "farewell test" even though it broke his heart (21:14-21).

Not every difficult experience in life is necessarily a personal test from God. (Of course, any experience could become a test or a temptation, depending on how we deal with it. See James 1:12-16.) Sometimes our own disobedience causes the pain or disappointment, as when Abraham went to Egypt (Gen. 12:10ff) and to Gerar (Gen. 20). Sometimes our hurts are simply a part of normal human life: As we grow older, friends and loved ones relocate or even die, life changes around us, and we must make painful adjustments.

Learn to distinguish between *trials* and *temptations.* Temptations come from our desires within us (James 1:12-16) while trials come from the Lord who has a special purpose to fulfill. Temptations are used by the devil to bring out the worst in us, but trials are used by the Holy Spirit to bring out the best in us (1:1-6). Temptations seem logical while trials seem very unreasonable. Why would God give Abraham a son and then ask Abraham to kill him?

All believers face similar temptations to sin (1 Cor. 10:13), but not all believers experience the same trials of faith. God's testings are tailor-made for each child of God, and each experience is unique. God never asked Lot to face the tests that Abraham faced. Why? Because Lot was being tempted by the world and the flesh and never grew to the place of maturity that Abraham reached. In one sense, it is a compliment when God sends us a test; it shows God wants to "promote us" in the "School of Faith." God never sends a test until He knows you are ready for it.

"Life is difficult," wrote psychiatrist M. Scott Peck. "Once we truly know that life is difficult—once we truly understand and accept it—then life is no longer difficult" (*The Road Less Traveled,* p. 15). That is the first lesson we must learn: Expect trials from God, because the Christian life is not easy.

2. Focus on promises, not explanations (Gen. 22:3-5)

"In the commencement of the spiritual life," wrote French mystic Madame Guyon, "our hardest task is to bear with our neighbor; in its progress, with ourselves; and in its end, with God." *Our faith is not really tested until God asks us to bear what seems unbearable, do what seems unreasonable, and expect what seems impossible.* Whether you look at Joseph in prison, Moses and Israel at the Red Sea, David in the cave, or Jesus at Calvary, the lesson is the same: We live by promises, not by explanations.

Consider how unreasonable God's request was. Isaac was Abraham's only son, and the future of the covenant rested in him. Isaac was a miracle child, the gift of God to Abraham and Sarah in response to their faith. Abraham and Sarah loved Isaac very much and had built their whole future around him. When God asked Abraham to offer his son, He was testing Abraham's faith, hope, and love; and it looked like God was wiping out everything Abraham and Sarah had lived for.

When God sends a trial to us, our first response is usually, "*Why,* Lord?" and then, "Why *me?*" Right away, we want God to give us explanations. Of course, we know that God has reasons for sending tests—perhaps to purify our faith (1 Peter 1:6-9), or perfect our character (James 1:1-4), or even to protect us from sin (2 Cor. 12:7-10)—but we fail to see how these things apply to us. The fact that we ask our Father for explanations suggests that we may not know ourselves as we should or God as we should.

Abraham heard God's word and immediately obeyed it by faith. He knew that God's will never contradicts God's promise, so he held on to the promise "in Isaac shall thy seed be called" (Gen. 21:12). Abraham believed that even if God allowed him to slay his son, He could raise Isaac from the dead (Heb. 11:17-19). *Faith does not demand explanations; faith rests on promises.*

Abraham told the two servants, "I and the lad will go yonder and worship, and come again to you" (Gen. 22:5). Because he believed God, Abraham had no intentions of bringing back a corpse! It has been pointed out that Abraham believed God and obeyed Him when he did not know *where*

(Heb. 11:8), when he did not know *when* (11:9-10, 13-16), when he did not know *how* (11:11-12), and when he did not know *why* (11:17-19).

3. Depend on God's provision (Gen. 22:6-14)

Two statements reveal the emphasis of this passage: "God will provide Himself a lamb for a burnt offering" (Gen. 22:8); and "Jehovah-jireh" (22:14), which means, "The Lord will see to it," that is, "The Lord will provide." As he climbed Mount Moriah with his son, Abraham was confident that God would meet every need.

On what could Abraham depend? He certainly could not depend on his feelings, for there must have been terrible pain within as he contemplated slaying his son on the altar. He loved his only son, but he also loved his God and wanted to obey Him.

Nor could Abraham depend on other people. Sarah was at home, and the two servants who accompanied him were back at the camp. We thank God for friends and family members who can help us carry our burdens, but there are some trials in life that we must face alone. *It is only then that we can see what our Father really can do for us!*

Abraham could depend on the promise and provision of the Lord. He had already experienced the resurrection power of God in his own body (Rom. 4:19-21), so he knew that God could raise Isaac from the dead if that was His plan. Apparently no resurrections had taken place before that time, so Abraham was exercising great faith in God.

According to Ephesians 1:19-20 and 3:20-21, believers today have Christ's resurrection power available in their own bodies as they yield to the Spirit of God. We can know "the power of His resurrection" (Phil. 3:10) as we face the daily demands and trials of life. When the situation appears to be hopeless, ask yourself, "Is anything too hard for the Lord?"

(Gen. 18:14) and remind yourself, "I can do all things through Christ who strengthens me" (Phil. 4:13, NKJV).

God did provide the sacrifice that was needed, and a ram took Isaac's place on the altar (Gen. 22:13). Abraham discovered a new name for God—"Jehovah-jireh"—which can be translated "The Lord will see to it" or "The Lord will be seen." The statement "In the mount of the Lord it shall be seen" helps us understand some truths about the provision of the Lord.

Where does the Lord provide our needs? In the place of His assignment. Abraham was at the right place, so God could meet his needs. We have no right to expect the provision of God if we are not in the will of God.

When does God meet our needs? Just when we have the need and not a minute before. When you bring your requests to the throne of grace, God answers with mercy and grace "in time of need" (Heb. 4:16). Sometimes it looks like God waits until the last minute to send help, but that is only from our human point of view. *God is never late.*

How does God provide for us? In ways that are usually quite natural. God did not send an angel with a sacrifice; He simply allowed a ram to get caught in a bush at a time when Abraham needed it and in a place where Abraham could get his hands on it. All Abraham needed was one animal, so God did not send a whole flock of sheep.

To whom does God give His provision? To those who trust Him and obey His instructions. When we are doing the will of God, we have the right to expect the provision of God. A deacon in the first church I pastored used to remind us, "When God's work is done in God's way, it will not lack God's support." God is not obligated to bless my ideas or projects, but He is obligated to support His work if it is done in His way.

Why does God provide our every need? For the great glory

of His name! "Hallowed be Thy name" is the first petition in the Lord's Prayer (Matt. 6:9-13), and it governs all the other requests. God was glorified on Mount Moriah because Abraham and Isaac did the will of the Lord and glorified Jesus Christ. We must pause to consider this important truth.

4. Seek to glorify Christ

In times of testing, it is easy to think only about *our* needs and *our* burdens; instead, we should be focusing on bringing glory to Jesus Christ. We find ourselves asking *"How* can I get out of this?" instead of *"What* can I get out of this that will honor the Lord?" We sometimes waste our sufferings by neglecting or ignoring opportunities to reveal Jesus Christ to others who are watching us go through the furnace.

If ever two suffering people revealed Jesus Christ, it was Abraham and Isaac on Mount Moriah. *Their experience is a picture of the Father and the Son and the cross* and is one of the most beautiful types of Christ found anywhere in the Old Testament. Jesus said to the Jews, "Your father, Abraham, rejoiced to see My day; and he saw it, and was glad" (John 8:56). In Isaac's miraculous birth, Abraham saw the day of Christ's birth; and in Isaac's marriage (Gen. 24), he saw the day of Christ's coming for His bride. But on Mount Moriah, when Isaac willingly put himself on the altar, Abraham saw the day of Christ's death and resurrection. Several truths about the atonement are seen in this event.

The Father and Son acted together. The touching phrase "they went both of them together" is found twice in the narrative (22:6, 8). In our evangelistic witness, we often emphasize the Father's love for lost sinners (John 3:16) and the Son's love for those for whom He died (1 John 3:16), but we fail to mention that the Father and the Son *love each other.* Jesus Christ is the Father's "beloved Son" (Matt. 3:17), and the Son said, "But that the world may know that I love the

Father" (John 14:31). Abraham did not withhold his son (Gen. 22:16), and the Father did not spare His Son but "delivered Him up for us all" (Rom. 8:32).

The Son had to die. Abraham carried a knife and a torch, both of them instruments of death. The knife would end Isaac's physical life, and the fire would burn the wood on the altar where his body lay. In Isaac's case, a substitute died for him; *but nobody could take the place of Jesus on the cross.* He was the only sacrifice that could finally and completely take away the sins of the world. God provided a *ram,* but Isaac had asked about a *lamb.* The answer to the question, "Where is the lamb?" was given by John the Baptist: "Behold the Lamb of God, who taketh away the sin of the world" (John 1:29).

In the Bible, fire often symbolizes the holiness of God (Deut. 4:24; 9:3; Heb. 12:29). The cross was the physical instrument of death; but at Calvary, Jesus experienced much more than death. He experienced the judgment of God for the sins of the world. Isaac felt neither the knife nor the fire, but Jesus felt both. Isaac's loving father was right there, but Jesus was forsaken by His Father when He became sin for us (Matt. 27:45-46; 2 Cor. 5:21). What marvelous love!

The Son bore the burden of sin. It is interesting that the wood is mentioned five times in the narrative and that Isaac did not start carrying the wood until he arrived at Mount Moriah. The wood is not a picture of the cross, for Jesus did not carry His cross all the way to Calvary. The wood seems to picture the burden of sin that Jesus bore for us (1 Peter 2:24). Abraham took the wood and "laid it upon Isaac his son" (Gen. 22:6), and "the Lord hath laid on Him [Jesus] the iniquity of us all" (Isa. 53:6). The fire consumed the wood as a picture of the judgment of God against sin.

The Son was raised from the dead. Isaac did not actually die, but "in a figurative sense" (Heb. 11:19, NKJV) he died and was raised from the dead. Jesus, however, really died, was buried, and was triumphantly resurrected. It is interesting that *Abraham* returned to the two servants (Gen. 22:19), *but nothing is said about Isaac.* In fact, Isaac is not mentioned again until he is seen meeting his bride (24:62). While it is obvious that Isaac did return home with his father, the Bible type reminds us that the next event on God's calendar is the return of Jesus Christ to claim His bride, the church.

The greatest thing that can happen as we experience the trials God sends is that we grow closer to our Father and become more like the Lord Jesus Christ. *Calvary is not only the place where Jesus died for our sins, but it is also the place where He sanctified suffering and, by His resurrection, transformed suffering into glory.* Seek to glorify the Lord, and He will do the rest.

Said Martin Luther: "Our suffering is not worthy [of] the name of suffering. When I consider my crosses, tribulations, and temptations, I shame myself almost to death, thinking what they are in comparison of the sufferings of my blessed Savior Christ Jesus."

5. Look forward to what God has for you (Gen. 22:15-24)
There is always an "afterward" to the tests of life (Heb. 12:11; 1 Peter 5:10), because God never wastes suffering. "But He knoweth the way that I take; when He hath tested me, I shall come forth as gold" (Job 23:10). Abraham received several blessings from God because of his obedient faith.

To begin with, he received *a new approval from God* (Gen. 22:12). Abraham had described this whole difficult experience as "worship" (22:5) because, to him, that is what it was. He obeyed God's will and sought to please God's heart, and God commended him. It is worth it to go through trials if, at the end, the Father can say to us, "Well done!"

He received back *a new son.* Isaac and Abraham had been at the altar together, and Isaac was now a "living sacrifice"

115

(Rom. 12:1-2). God gave Isaac to Abraham, and Abraham gave Isaac back to God. *We must be careful that God's gifts do not take the place of the Giver.*

God gave Abraham *new assurances* (Gen. 22:16-18). He had heard these promises before, but now they took on fresh new meaning. Charles Spurgeon used to say that the promises of God never shine brighter than in the furnace of affliction. What two men did on a lonely altar would one day bring blessing to the whole world!

Abraham also learned a *new name for God* (22:14). As we have seen, Jehovah-jireh means "the Lord will be seen" or "the Lord will see to it [provide]." The Jewish temple was built on Mount Moriah (2 Chron. 3:1); and during our Lord's earthly ministry, He was seen there. He was the true Lamb of God, provided by God to die for the sins of the world.

The founder of the China Inland Mission (now the Overseas Missionary Fellowship), J. Hudson Taylor, used to hang in his home a plaque with two Hebrew words on it: "Ebenezer" and "Jehovah-jireh." They mean: "Hitherto hath the Lord helped us" (1 Sam. 7:12) and "The Lord will see to it." Whether he looked back or ahead, Hudson Taylor knew the Lord was at work, and he had nothing to fear.

When he arrived back home, Abraham heard another new name—Rebekah (Gen. 22:23)—the girl God was saving for Isaac. The roll call of the names of Abraham's brother's family could have discouraged a man with only one son, but Abraham did not fret. After all, he had God's promise that his descendants would be as numerous as the stars in the sky and the sand on the seashore! (22:17)

Finally, Abraham came away from this trial with *a deeper love for the Lord.* Jesus tells us about this deeper love in John 14:21-24, and Paul prays about it in Ephesians 3:14-21. Have you experienced it?

march 13
Jim

Here Comes the Bride!

It seems strange that the longest chapter in Genesis tells the story of how a man got his wife. While that is an important topic, and this is certainly a beautiful story, does it deserve that much space? Only thirty-one verses are devoted to the Creation account in Genesis 1; sixty-seven verses are allowed to relate how Rebekah became Isaac's wife. Why?

For one thing, the chapter emphasizes *separation.* Abraham made it clear that his son was not to marry a Canaanite woman (24:3). The Law of Moses did not permit the Jewish men to marry heathen women (Deut. 7:1-11). Nor are believers today to marry unbelievers (2 Cor. 6:14-18; 1 Cor. 7:39-40). Genesis 24 is a great encouragement for those who want God's will in the selection of a mate. Today, while we do not use the same manner as Abraham's servant, the principles still apply: We must want God's will, we must pray and seek His guidance, we must be willing to obey, and we must be alert to what God is doing.

Of course, when the husband in the story is Isaac, the beloved son of Abraham, then the narrative takes on greater significance. After all, Isaac was the next "living link" in the chain of blessing that culminated in the birth of the Savior,

Jesus Christ; so whatever happens to Isaac is of utmost importance in God's great plan of salvation.

But the chapter goes beyond history into theology. It gives us a picture of the Heavenly Father getting a bride for His Son (Matt. 22:1-14). The church is compared to a bride (2 Cor. 11:2-3; Eph. 5:22-33); and during this present age, the Holy Spirit is calling people to trust Christ and be "married to . . . Him" (Rom. 7:4). The elements involved in the marriage of Isaac and Rebekah are also involved in the marriage of Christ and His church. There are four of them.

1. The will of the father (Gen. 24:1-9)

Abraham was now 140 years old (Gen. 21:5; 25:20) and would live another 35 years (25:7). His great concern was that, before he died, he would find a wife for his only son Isaac. Only then could God fulfill His covenant promises to bless Abraham with many descendants and give them Canaan for their inheritance (12:1-3; 13:14-17; 15:18; 21:12). In those days, the parents made the marriage arrangements. A man and woman got married and then learned to love each other (24:67). In much of the world today, the pattern is different.

We do not know who this "eldest servant" was. If it was Eliezer (15:2), then he must have been very old; the events recorded in Genesis 15 occurred more than fifty years earlier. Abraham made him swear to three things: (1) he would not select a wife for Isaac from among the Canaanite women; (2) he would choose her from Abraham's relatives; and (3) he would not take Isaac back to Abraham's former home.

Knowing that he had assigned his servant a difficult task, Abraham also gave him some words of encouragement (24:7, 39-41). God had guided and blessed Abraham for sixty-five years and would not forsake him now. Furthermore, God had given Abraham a specific promise that his seed would inherit the land; so this meant that his son had to have a wife who would bear him a child. Finally, God's angel would go before the servant and guide him to the right woman.

Abraham was a man of faith who believed God's word and knew how to apply it to specific situations and decisions. He sought to obey God's word because true faith always results in obedience. The more you meditate on God's Word, the more truth you will see in it and the more direction you will get from it. This applies to decisions about marriage, vocation, ministry, or any other area in life. Unless we trust God's Word and obey it, He will not direct us (Prov. 3:5-6).

Just as Abraham wanted a bride for his son, so God the Father elected to provide a bride for His beloved Son. Why? Not because Jesus needed anything, for the eternal Son of God is self-existent and self-sufficient and needs nothing. *The bride is the Father's love gift to His Son.* We usually emphasize that the Son is the Father's love gift to the world (John 3:16) and forget that the church is the Father's love gift to His Son (17:2, 6, 9, 11-12, 24).

In the divine counsels of eternity, the Father elected to save lost sinners by His grace, the Son agreed to die for the sins of the world, and the Holy Spirit agreed to apply that work to the lives of all who would believe. This is revealed in Ephesians 1:1-14, where you see the work of God the Father (1:3-6), God the Son (1:7-12), and God the Holy Spirit (1:13-14). Note especially that the reason for this great plan of salvation is *the glory of God* (1:6, 12, 14). Those who trusted Christ would be a special people, His inheritance (1:18) and His bride (5:22-33). His bride would bring glory to Christ on earth and throughout all eternity. One day Jesus Christ would have the joy of presenting His bride in glory to the Father (Heb. 12:2; Jude 24).

The next time you have the privilege of witnessing for Jesus Christ, remember that you are inviting people to come to the wedding!

2. The witness of the servant (Gen. 24:10-49)

The servant. Neither Abraham nor Isaac went to find the bride; the task was given to an anonymous servant, who was completely devoted to Abraham. His favorite name for Abraham was "my master," which he used nineteen times in this narrative. He lived and served only to please his master, and that is a good example for us to follow today.

The servant got his orders from his master and did not change them. When he made his vow of obedience, he meant it and kept it. Whether his mission succeeded or failed, the servant knew he would have to give an account to his master; and he wanted to be able to do so without embarrassment. (See Rom. 14:10-12 and 1 John 2:28.)

But how would he go about finding the right woman for his master's son? *The servant acted by faith in the God of Abraham and Isaac (Gen. 24:12).* He believed the promise of God and trusted the providence of God to direct him (24:27). He took time to pray and to ask God for help, and he kept his eyes open to see what God might do. In fact, while he was praying, God was sending the answer (Isa. 65:24). The servant was not impulsive but waited on the Lord to see what He might do (Gen. 24:21). "Whoever believes will not act hastily" (Isa. 28:16, NKJV).

The bride. In His providence, God brought Rebekah to the well just as the servant was praying; and she did exactly what the servant had been praying about. The servant did what Gideon would do years later, "put out a fleece" (Jud. 6:36-40). This is not the best way for God's people to determine the will of God, because the conditions we lay down for God to meet might not be in His will. We are walking by sight and not by faith, and we may end up tempting God. However, God accommodated Himself to the needs of the servant (and Gideon) and guided them as they requested.

Little did Rebekah know that doing a humble task for a

stranger would make her the bride of a wealthy man who was in a covenant relationship with God. She would become the mother of Jacob, and he would become the father of the twelve tribes of Israel! Years ago, I read a quotation from a writer identified only as "Marsden," and it has stuck with me: "Make every occasion a great occasion, for you can never tell when someone may be taking your measure for a larger place."

The servant was evaluating Rebekah to see if she would make a good wife for Isaac. He could see that she was kind, pleasant, humble, healthy, and a hard worker. Watering ten camels is no easy job! After a long trek, a thirsty camel might drink as much as forty gallons of water; and Rebekah had to draw all that water by hand.

"Whose daughter art thou?" (Gen. 24:23) is a key question for any suitor to ask. Of course, the servant was interested in her family, but the question has a wider application for Christian believers today, both men and women. "Are you a child of God? Have you been born again into the family of God?" What a tragedy when believers marry unbelievers and try to establish a home without the full blessing of God.

The family. Rebekah took her gifts and ran home to tell her father, mother, and brother Laban (who seemed to be the leader in the home) that a generous stranger needed a place to stay for the night. Hospitality is the first law of the East, so the family went out to meet the visitor. Laban's character is revealed in 24:30: He was more excited about the expensive gifts than the privilege of showing hospitality to a stranger. Isaac and Rebekah's son Jacob would discover years later what a clever rogue Laban really was (Gen. 29–31).

The servant would not eat until he had fulfilled his mission (24:33; John 4:32). He did not speak about himself but about Isaac and his great wealth. (The train of ten camels helped to tell the story.) He reviewed his experience at the well, and for the first time Rebekah discovered that she had been "measured" for a new and exciting assignment. But, would they let her go, and would she be willing to go?

Before we learn the answer to those questions, we must pause to see how the servant illustrates the work of the Holy Spirit in the world today as He uses us to witness about Jesus Christ (Acts 1:8). He did not speak about himself but about his master and his riches (John 15:26; 16:13-14). He gave tokens of his master's wealth just as the Spirit gives us the "firstfruits" and "down payment" of our spiritual riches in Christ (Eph. 1:13-14). The best is yet to come!

The servant's job was not to argue or bribe but simply to bear witness to the greatness of his master. He did not force Rebekah to marry Isaac; he merely gave her the facts and the opportunity to make a decision. While there is nothing wrong with urging people to be saved (Acts 2:40), we must be careful not to try to take the place of the Spirit who alone can do the work of conviction in the human heart (John 16:7-11).

3. The willingness of the bride (Gen. 24:50-60)

Rebekah's brother and mother were willing for her to become Isaac's wife, but they wanted her to wait at least ten days before leaving home. This was a natural request, since the parents would want to spend as much time as possible with her and perhaps even invite the neighbors to celebrate with them (31:25-27). Of course, they were delighted with the wealth the servant gave them, which was probably the marriage dowry; and no doubt they wanted to hear more about Isaac and the home Rebekah would share with him.

Just as the servant would not delay in presenting his petition (24:33), so he would not delay in completing his mission. When the Lord is at work, that is the time to keep going! He asked that they let Rebekah make the choice, and her reply was, "I will go." This is the decision every sinner must make if he or she is to be "married to Christ" and share His home in heaven.

What motivated Rebekah to make the right decision? She heard the word about Isaac and believed it. She saw the proof of his greatness, generosity, and wealth and wanted to belong to him for the rest of her life. She had never seen Isaac (1 Peter 1:8), but what she had heard about him convinced her to go to Canaan with the servant.

Her parents and friends could have given Rebekah many arguments for waiting or even for saying no. "You have never seen the man!" "Maybe the servant is a fraud!" "It's nearly 500 miles to where Isaac lives. That's a long trip!" "You may never see your family again!" But she was determined to make the long, difficult journey and become the wife of a man she knew only by hearsay.

The application is obvious for unsaved people today: *They must not delay in making their decisions for Christ.* It is a decision of faith, based on the evidence provided by the Holy Spirit through the Word and the witness of the church. The sinner who delays is in danger of losing the opportunity to belong to God's family and live in heaven (John 14:1-6). "Today, if you will hear His voice, do not harden your hearts" (Heb. 3:7, 15, NKJV). "Behold, now is the accepted time; behold, now is the day of salvation" (2 Cor. 6:2).

At the closing service of a great evangelistic crusade he conducted in Fort Worth, Texas, Dr. George W. Truett, then pastor of First Baptist Church of Dallas, said to a vast congregation: "Satan does not care if men and women come to the house of God, and to public services such as these, and are attentive and serious and deeply moved, if only they will let the religious opportunity pass, and be unimproved. Oh, dreadful possibility, that religious opportunity may come and pass by, and the highest things of the soul be lost and forfeited forever" (*A Quest for Souls,* p. 362). Dreadful possibility indeed!

A century and a half before, Charles Spurgeon said to his London congregation: "Ten days did not seem too long; but they might have been ten days too late. One day does not seem much; but one day more may be one day too late, and one day too late is to be too late forever; yea, one minute too late is an eternity too late!" (*Metropolitan Tabernacle Pulpit,* vol. 13, p. 533)

The entire story makes it clear that God had chosen Rebekah for Isaac, for His providential leading is seen each step of the way. *Yet Rebekah had to make her choice of Isaac.* There is no conflict between divine sovereignty (God's plan) and human responsibility (man's choice). In fact, Jesus taught *both* in one statement: "All that the Father giveth Me shall come to Me [divine sovereignty], and him that cometh to Me [human responsibility] I will in no wise cast out" (John 6:37).

"Am I one of God's elect?" is not the question the lost sinner should ask. The admonition to "make your calling and election sure" was written to believers (2 Peter 1:10), not to lost sinners. The question the lost sinner should ask is, "What must I do to be saved?" (Acts 16:30; cf. 2:37) And the answer is, "Believe on the Lord Jesus Christ" (16:31). When God is speaking to you, that is the time to respond and put your faith in Christ (Isa. 55:6-7).

"We make our decisions," wrote Frank Boreham, "and then our decisions turn around and make us." From the minute she left her home (Gen. 35:8), Rebekah was under the special providential care of God and was now a part of a thrilling plan that would bring salvation to the whole world (12:1-3). Had she stayed in Mesopotamia and married one of the local men, we would never have heard of her again.

4. The welcome of the bridegroom (Gen. 24:61-67)
Camels traveled about 25 miles a day and could cover 60 miles if they had to, while the average pedestrian walked

about 20 miles a day. A train of 10 camels with its attendants and guards could easily make the trip from Hebron to Mesopotamia and back (about 900 miles) in less than 2 months. The servant was the kind of man who permitted no delay and was anxious to complete his task successfully. Certainly Abraham and Isaac were both praying for him and his mission, and their prayers were answered.

Isaac pictures our Lord Jesus Christ in his miraculous birth (Gen. 21) and in his willingness to obey his father and give his life (Gen. 22). We have already noticed that Genesis 22:19 does not tell us that Isaac returned with his father from Mount Moriah, although certainly he did (22:5). This omission suggests the ascension of our Lord: He returned to glory to wait for the time to receive His bride (1 Thes. 4:13-18).

Isaac was not living with his father at that time but was south of Hebron, getting ready to establish his own home. Isaac is identified with *wells* (Gen. 24:62; 25:11; 26:17-33) just as Abraham is identified with *altars*. Water was a precious commodity and had to be guarded carefully.

The name of the well would be an encouragement to Isaac as he waited for the return of the servant: "the well of Him who lives and sees me" (16:14). If God took care of Hagar and met her needs, surely He would take care of Isaac and provide the wife that he needed in order to maintain the messianic line. Jehovah is the Living God who sees everything and plans all things for His glory and the good of His children.

Genesis 24:63 suggests that Isaac was a quiet, meditative man who pondered the things of the Lord in solitude (Ps. 1:2). His wife was more the activist type, so there would be a good balance in their home. The two saw each other at a distance, and Rebekah dismounted so she could meet him on foot. In that day, it was considered a breach of etiquette if women rode beasts in the presence of strange men. She also put on the long veil that was a mark of her modesty and submission.

It is significant that Isaac met his bride "at the eventide" (Gen. 24:63); for when Jesus comes for His church, it will be a time of spiritual darkness (Rom. 13:11-14). Just as a new day dawned for Rebekah, so also will the coming of Jesus Christ usher in a new day for His people (1 Thes. 5:1-11).

But that meeting involved much more than the claiming of the bride by the bridegroom. The servant also gave an account of himself to his master's son (Gen. 24:66). When Jesus Christ comes for His church, there will not only be a joyful wedding (Rev. 19:1-9) but also a solemn judgment seat (Rom. 14:10-13; 2 Cor. 5:9-10) where our works will be examined and rewards given out (1 Cor. 3:13-15; 4:1-5).

With Isaac, it was "love at first sight"; but what did Jesus Christ see in *us* that He should want *us* to be His bride? We were rebellious sinners with no beauty or merit to boast about, and yet Jesus loved us and died for us (Rom. 5:6-8).

Rebekah had received a few gifts from Isaac; but now that she was his very own, she possessed everything that he possessed. Their lives were one, and so it is with Christ and His church (Eph. 5:22-33).

This is much more than an ancient, idyllic love story. It can be *your* love story *today* if you trust Jesus Christ and say, "I will go!"

If you already belong to Jesus Christ, then be like the faithful servant and tell others the good news about the marriage and the glorious wedding feast yet to come. Invite them to say, "I will go!"

march 20 +5

"*A Time to Die*"

King Solomon said, "A good name is better than precious ointment; and the day of death, than the day of one's birth" (Ecc. 7:1). He did not say that death is better than birth; for, after all, we must be born before we can die.

Solomon's point was that *the name* given you at birth is like fragrant ointment, *and you must keep it that way until you die.* When you received your name at birth, nobody knew what you would make out of it; but at death, that name is either fragrant or putrid. If it is fragrant at death, then people can rejoice; for after death, nothing can change it. So, for a person with a good name, the day of death is better than the day of birth.

The names of Abraham and Sarah were fragrant in life and in death and are still fragrant today. In these chapters, we meet Abraham and Sarah at the end of life's road, and we learn from them what it means to die in faith.

1. The death of a princess (Gen. 23:1-20)

Sarah had been a good wife to Abraham and a good mother to Isaac. Yes, she had her faults, as we all do; but God called her a princess (Gen. 17:15) and listed her with the heroes and heroines of faith (Heb. 11:11). The Apostle Peter named her as a good example for Christian wives to follow (1 Peter 3:1-6), and Paul used her to illustrate the grace of God in the life of the believer (Gal. 4:21-31).

Abraham's tears (Gen. 23:1-2). How often in my pastoral ministry I have heard well-meaning but ignorant people say to grieving friends or relatives, "Now, don't cry!" That is very poor counsel, for God made us with the ability to weep; and He expects us to cry. Even Jesus wept (John 11:35). Grieving is one of God's gifts to help heal broken hearts when people we love are taken from us in death. Paul did not tell the Thessalonian Christians not to weep; he cautioned them not to sorrow "as others who have no hope" (1 Thes. 4:13-18). The grief of a believer should be different from that of an unbeliever.

Abraham loved his wife, and her death was a painful experience for him. He showed his love and his grief by his weeping. These are the first recorded tears in the Bible, and tears will not end until God wipes them away in glory (Rev. 21:4). Even though he was a man of faith, Abraham did not feel that his tears were an evidence of unbelief.

Sarah died in faith (Heb. 11:11, 13), so Abraham knew that she was in the Lord's care. In the Old Testament, very little was revealed about the afterlife; but God's people knew that God would receive them when they died (Ps. 73:24).

The late Vance Havner had a wife named Sarah. Shortly after her untimely death, I was with Dr. Havner at the Moody Bible Institute, and I shared my condolences with him.

"I'm sorry to hear you lost your wife," I said to him when we met in the dining room.

He smiled and replied, "Son, when you know where something is, *you haven't lost it.*"

For the believer, to be "absent from the body" means to be "present with the Lord" (Phil. 1:21-23; 2 Cor. 5:1-8); so

Christians do not approach death with fear. "Blessed are the dead which die in the Lord . . . that they may rest from their labors; and their works do follow them" (Rev. 14:13).

The death of the wicked is vividly described in Job 18, and what a fearful picture it is! When the wicked die, it is like putting out a light (18:5-6), trapping an animal or a bird (18:7-10), catching a criminal (18:11-14), or uprooting a tree (18:15-21). What a difference it makes when you know Jesus Christ as your Savior and as "the resurrection and the life" (John 11:25-26; 2 Tim. 1:10).

Abraham's testimony (Gen. 23:3-6). We cannot mourn over our dead forever; there comes a time when we must accept what has happened, face life, and fulfill our obligations to both the living and the dead. Because he was not a citizen of the land (Heb. 11:13), Abraham had to request a place to bury his wife. The truth was that Abraham owned the whole land. God had given it to him, but there was no way he could convince his neighbors of that.

Like Abraham, God's people today are "pilgrims and strangers" in this present world (1 Peter 1:1; 2:11). We live in "tents" (2 Cor. 5:1-8) which one day will be taken down when we move to glory. When Paul wrote "the time of my departure is at hand" (2 Tim. 4:6), he used a military word that meant "to take down a tent and move on." Our present body is temporary, but one day we will receive a glorified body like the body that Jesus Christ now has in heaven (Phil. 3:20-21; 1 John 3:1-3).

The men of the land called Abraham "a mighty prince" (Gen. 23:6), which in the Hebrew is "a prince with God." He had a good testimony among them, and they respected him. Even though this world is not our home, we must be careful as pilgrims and strangers to have a good witness to those who are outside the faith (1 Thes. 4:12; Col. 4:5; 1 Peter 2:11ff). These Hittites did not worship Abraham's God, but they respected Abraham and his faith. In fact, they offered him the use of one of their own tombs (Gen. 23:6); but Abraham refused.

It is a wonderful thing in a time of sorrow when the child of God has a strong witness to the lost. There is a natural sorrow that everyone expects us to manifest, but there is also a supernatural grace that God gives so that we might have joy in the midst of sorrow. The unsaved can tell the difference, and this gives us opportunity for sharing the good news of the Gospel.

Abraham's tact (Gen. 23:7-16). In the East in that day, most business transactions were carried on at the city gate (23:10) with the people as witnesses (23:7). Arriving at a final price for a piece of property usually involved a great deal of bargaining and deferential politeness that sometimes covered up greed and intrigue. But Abraham was open and honest in his request: He wanted to buy the cave of Machpelah from Ephron, who was in the crowd at the time.

Following the custom of the East, Ephron offered to give Abraham not only the cave but the whole field in which the cave was located. Of course, this was only a clever maneuver on his part; for he had no intentions of giving away a valuable piece of property, especially to a man as wealthy as Abraham. But Ephron's reply gave Abraham two pieces of information: Ephron was willing to sell, but he wanted to sell the whole field and not just the cave.

Ephron had Abraham in a corner, and he knew it. Sarah had to be buried soon, and Ephron had the only piece of property that met Abraham's needs. So, Abraham agreed to buy both the cave and the field even before Ephron named the price. That is really living by faith! Ephron's price was far too much, but Abraham paid it and claimed the property for himself.

In Acts 7:15-16, Stephen seems to contradict the Genesis

record by saying that Abraham bought the property from Hamor and it was located in Shechem rather than Hebron (Gen. 23:19). But surely two different burial places are in view here. It is likely that Abraham bought a second burial plot from Hamor in Shechem and that Jacob had to buy it back years later (33:18-19). Since Abraham, Isaac, and Jacob moved about quite a bit, it would be difficult for the residents of the land to keep track of them and their family real estate.

In our business dealings with the people of the world, we must be careful to maintain honesty and integrity and to put our witness for the Lord ahead of monetary gain. Abraham knew that Ephron had him trapped and that it was foolish to haggle over the price, as much as Easterners love to do it.

Abraham's tomb (Gen. 23:17-20). The key phrase in the chapter, used seven times, is "bury my [the, thy] dead." Even though Sarah was gone, Abraham showed respect for her body and wanted to give it a proper burial. This is the pattern for God's people throughout the Scriptures. Neither the Old Testament Jews nor the New Testament Christians cremated their dead. Rather, they washed the body, wrapped it in clean cloth with spices, and placed it in the ground or in a tomb. While there may be some situations when cremation is the better way to dispose of the body, for the most part, Christians prefer burial. This is the way our Lord's body was handled after His death (Matt. 27:57-61), and Paul seems to teach burial in 1 Corinthians 15:35-46.

When Abraham purchased the cave of Machpelah for a tomb, he was making a statement of faith to all who were there. He did not take Sarah back to their former home in Ur but buried her in the land God had given him and his descendants. He did not ignore the body but gave it a proper burial *in view of the promised resurrection.* When God saves us, He saves the whole person, not just "the soul." The body has a future, and burial bears witness to our faith in the return of

Christ and the resurrection of the body.

It must be pointed out, however, that resurrection is not "reconstruction." God will not reassemble the dust of the body and restore the body to its previous state. God promises us a new body! In 1 Corinthians 15:35-38, Paul makes it clear that there is *continuity* but not *identity* between the old body and the new body.

He illustrated this miracle with the planting of a seed. The seed dies and decays, but from it comes a beautiful flower or some grain. There is continuity but not identity: The same seed does not come out of the ground, but what came out came from the seed that was planted. Christian burial bears witness that we believe in a future resurrection.

When you get to the end of Genesis, you find that Abraham's tomb is quite full. Sarah was buried there, and then Abraham, Isaac, Rebekah, and Leah (Gen. 49:29-31); and then Jacob joined them (50:13). Genesis ends with a full tomb, but the four Gospels end with an *empty* tomb! Jesus has conquered death and taken away its sting (1 Cor. 15:55-58). Because of His victory, we need not fear death or the grave.

Abraham owned the whole land, but the only piece of property that was legally his was *a tomb.* If the Lord Jesus does not return to take us to heaven, *the only piece of property each of us will own in this world will be a plot in the cemetery!* We will take nothing with us; we will leave it all behind (1 Tim. 6:7). But, if we are investing in things eternal, we can send it ahead (Matt. 6:19-34). If we live by faith, then we can die by faith; and when you die by faith, you have a wonderful future.

In November 1858, missionary John Paton landed in the New Hebrides to establish a ministry among the people. On February 12, 1859, his wife gave birth to a son; and on March 3, his wife died. Seventeen days later, the baby died. "But for Jesus and the fellowship He gave me there," said Paton, "I must have gone mad and died beside that lonely grave."

But we do not sorrow as those who have no hope! We have been born again "to a living hope through the resurrection of Jesus Christ from the dead" (1 Peter 1:3, NKJV), and we are "looking for that blessed hope, and the glorious appearing of the great God and our Savior Jesus Christ" (Titus 2:13).

2. The death of a patriarch (Gen. 25:1-11)

After a person dies, we read the obituary; and after the burial, we read the will. Let's do that with Abraham.

Abraham's obituary (Gen. 25:7-8). He died "in a good old age" as the Lord had promised him (15:15). He had walked with the Lord for a century (12:4) and had been "the friend of God" (James 2:23). Old age is "good" if you have the blessing of the Lord on your life (Prov. 16:31). In spite of physical deterioration and weakness, you can enjoy His presence and do His will until the very end (2 Cor. 4:16–5:8).

Like Sarah before him, Abraham "died in faith." For 100 years, he had been a stranger and a pilgrim on the earth, seeking a heavenly country; and now his desires were fulfilled (Heb. 11:13-16). His life had not been an easy one; but he had walked by faith a day at a time, and the Lord had brought him through. Whenever Abraham failed the Lord, he returned to Him and started over again; and the Lord gave him a new beginning.

He also died "full of years" (Gen. 25:8). This suggests more than a quantity of time; it suggests a quality of life. James Strahan translates it "satisfied with life" (*Hebrew Ideals*, p. 197). Abraham, who was flourishing and fruitful to the very end, fulfilled the picture of old age given in Psalm 92:12-15. How few people really experience joy and satisfaction when they reach old age! When they look back, it is with regret; when they look ahead, it is with fear; and when they look around, it is with complaint.

An anonymous wit claimed that he would rather be "over

the hill" than under it. But death is not a threat to the person who trusts Jesus Christ and lives by His Word. Old age can be a time of rich experience in the Lord and wonderful opportunities to share Him with the next generation (Pss. 48:13-14; 78:5-7). Then, when death comes, you go to meet the Lord with joyful confidence.

God promised that Abraham would die "in peace" (Gen. 15:15), and he did. Welsh poet Dylan Thomas wrote that "old age should burn and rave at close of day"; but that is not the Christian approach to old age or death. Abraham was saved by faith (15:6), so he had "peace with God" (Rom. 5:1). He had walked in the way of righteousness, so he experienced the peace of God (Isa. 32:17). The God who had guided him for a century would not forsake him at the very end (46:4).

Like everything else in life, to be successful in old age, you must start working at it very young. That is the counsel Solomon gives in Ecclesiastes 12. The chapter describes some of the inevitable physical problems of old age, but it also emphasizes that a godly life *beginning in one's youth* is an investment that pays rich dividends when life draws to a close.

The phrase "gathered to his people" (Gen. 25:8) does not mean "buried with the family"; for Sarah's body was the only one in the family tomb. This is the first occurrence of this phrase in the Bible; and it means to go to the realm of the dead, referring to the destiny of the spirit, not the body (James 2:26). The Old Testament word for the realm of the dead is *sheol;* the New Testament equivalent is *hades.* It is the temporary "home" of the spirits of the dead awaiting the resurrection (Rev. 20:11-15).

The permanent home for the saved is heaven; and for the lost, it is hell. Luke 16:19-31 indicates that sheol-hades has two sections to it, separated by a great gulf; and that the saved are in a place of blessing while the lost are in a place of pain. It is likely that Jesus emptied the paradise portion of sheol-hades when He returned to heaven in glory (Eph. 4:8-10). The punishment portion of hades will be emptied at the resurrection that precedes the judgment of the Great White Throne (Rev. 20:11-15). For the lost, hades is the jail, while hell is the penitentiary.

One day, you will be "gathered to your people." If God's people were your people in life, then you will be with them after death in the home that Jesus is now preparing (John 14:1-6). If the Christian family is not your "people," then you will be with the crowd that is going to hell; and it is described in Revelation 21:8, 27. You had better make the right choice, because eternity is forever.

Abraham's will (Gen. 25:1-6). Abraham left his material wealth to his family and his spiritual wealth to the whole world, all who would believe on Jesus Christ.

When God renewed Abraham's natural strength for the begetting of Isaac, He did not take that strength away; and Abraham was able to marry again and have another family. However, he made a distinction between these six new sons and his son Isaac; for Isaac was God's choice to carry on the covenant line. Keturah's sons received gifts, but Isaac received the inheritance and the blessings of the covenant.

All who have trusted Jesus Christ are "as Isaac was, the children of promise" (Gal. 4:28). This means that we have a share in Abraham's will! What did he leave us?

To begin with, Abraham left us *a clear witness of salvation through faith.* Paul cited his example in Romans 4:1-5, relating it to Abraham's experience in Genesis 15. Abraham could not have been saved by keeping the Law because the Law had not yet been given. He could not have been saved by the ritual of circumcision because God declared him to be righteous long before Abraham was circumcised. Like everybody else who has ever been saved, Abraham was saved by faith and by faith alone. (See Heb. 11 and Gal. 3.)

But Abraham also leaves us *the example of a faithful life.* James used Abraham to illustrate the importance of proving our faith by our works (James 2:14-26). Wherever Abraham went, he pitched his tent and built his altar; and he let the people of the land know that he was a worshiper of the true and living God. When he offered Isaac on the altar, Abraham proved his faith in God and his love for God. He was not saved by works, but he proved his faith by his works.

From Abraham, we learn *how to walk by faith.* True, he had his occasional lapses of faith; but the general manner of his life evidenced faith in God's Word. "By faith Abraham . . . obeyed" (Heb. 11:8). "The pith, the essence of faith," said Charles Spurgeon, "lies in this: a casting oneself on the promises."

The late composer-conductor Leonard Bernstein said to an interviewer, "I believe in everything, in anything that anybody believes in, because I believe in people. In other words, I believe in belief. I believe in faith" (*Maestro: Encounters With Conductors of Today,* by Helena Matheopoulos; Harper & Row, 1982; p. 7).

But "faith in faith" is not the same as faith in God, because it has no foundation. It is building on the sand (Matt. 7:24-27). *True faith is our obedient response to the Word of God.* God speaks, we hear Him and believe, and we do what He tells us to do. Abraham and Sarah held on to God's promises and God rewarded their faith.

Abraham gave the world *the gift of the Jewish nation;* and it is through the Jews that we have the knowledge of the true God plus the Word of God and the salvation of God (John 4:22). It is beyond my understanding how anybody could be anti-Semitic when the Jews have given so much to the world and have suffered so much in this world. It is unfortunate that the Jewish people thought their relationship to Abraham saved them (Matt. 3:7-12; John 8:33-59), but they are no different from unsaved Gentiles who think they are going to heaven because their parents or grandparents were Christians (John 1:11-13).

Finally, because of Abraham, *we have a Savior.* In the first verse of the New Testament (Matt. 1:1), Abraham's name is joined with the names of David and Jesus Christ! God promised Abraham that through him all the world would be blessed (Gen. 12:1-3), and He has kept that promise. The problem is that the church is not telling the whole world that Jesus is indeed "the Savior of the world" (John 4:42). We are keeping the good news to ourselves when we ought to be doing everything we can to let the whole world know.

There can be only one Abraham and Sarah in God's great plan of redemption, but you and I have our tasks to perform in the will of God (Eph. 2:10). *Today,* you are writing your obituary and preparing your "last will and testament" as far as your spiritual heritage is concerned. *Today* you are getting ready for the last stage of life's journey.

Are you making good preparations?

Are you living by faith?

If you live by faith, then you will, like Abraham, BE OBEDIENT.

Chapter One

A New Beginning
(Genesis 11:27–12:9)

1. Why did God call Abraham?

2. How is Abraham's life an example for Christians today?

3. On what is true faith based?

4. What did God promise Abraham?

5. What are some promises God has given us?

6. How did Abraham not obey God completely?

7. How did Abraham show that he trusted God?

8. What does Abraham's response to God teach us about faith?

9. In what areas of your life do you need more faith in God?

10. How can you "build up" your faith?

Chapter Ten

The Greatest Test of All
(Genesis 22)

1. Is every difficult experience a test from God? Why or why not?

2. What were some of the other tests that Abraham faced before God asked him to sacrifice Isaac?

3. What's the difference between trials and temptations?

4. Does every Christian have trials from God? Why?

5. What does it mean for a Christian to focus on promises, not explanations?

6. What is usually our first concern when we're being tested? What should our first concern be?

7. How is this story of Abraham and Isaac at Mount Moriah a picture of Jesus' death for us?

8. What is the main difference between this story and Jesus' death?

9. What does God's name, "Jehovah-Jireh," mean to you?

10. Have you gone or are you going through a time of testing from the Lord? Share what the Lord has taught you.

Chapter Eleven

Here Comes the Bride!
(Genesis 24)

1. Why is the story of Isaac getting a bride so important?

2. What does this story teach the Christian about choosing a husband or wife?

3. Who is the bride that God has provided for His Son? Explain.

4. How did Abraham encourage his servant for what seemed an impossible task?

5. In what ways is Abraham's servant a good example for Christians to follow today?

6. God answered the servant's prayer at the well before he even finished praying! When has that happened to you? Describe.

7. How does the servant illustrate the work of the Holy Spirit today?

8. How is Rebekah a good example of always doing your best no matter what the job?

9. What are some similarities between Isaac and Rebekah and Christ and His church?

10. How is the servant's response, when he met Rebekah, an example for us today?

Chapter Twelve

A *Time to Die*
(Genesis 23; 25:1-11)

1. How is the grief of a believer different from that of an unbeliever?

2. How are Christians "pilgrims and strangers" in this world?

3. What should a Christian's business dealings be like? Give examples from your own experience.

4. How does a Christian burial demonstrate our belief in a future resurrection?

5. What do you think of the "American" funeral? Do you think God is glorified by it?

6. What are some ways God can use us in our old age?

7. What is the difference between hades and hell?

8. "All who have trusted Jesus Christ are as Isaac was, the children of promise." What does that mean to you?

9. What do Christians today owe to Abraham?

10. What would you like your epitaph to say?